The Gentle Art of Mentoring

Donna Ott[...]

HARVEST HOUSE PUBLISHERS
Eugene, Oregon 97402

Cover by Terry Dugan Design, Minneapolis, Minnesota

THE GENTLE ART OF MENTORING

Copyright © 1997 by Donna Otto
Published by Harvest House Publishers
Eugene, Oregon 97402

Library of Congress Cataloging-in-Publication Data

Otto, Donna.
    The gentle art of mentoring / Donna Otto.
       p. cm.
    ISBN 1-56507-757-1
    1. Christian women—Religious life—Study and teaching. 2. Church work with women—Study and teaching. 3. Mentoring in church work—Study and teaching. 4. Christian life—Study and teaching.
    I. Title.
    BV4527.O88 1997
    253'.7—dc21   97-2658
                                                          CIP

Printed in the United States of America.

97 98 99 00 01 02 / BP / 10 9 8 7 6 5 4 3 2 1

❧ *Acknowledgments* ☙

Scottsdale Bible Church
Dr. Darryl DelHousaye
Daisy Hepburn
Carol Drew
Diane Fuhr
Mentors for Mothers Staff
Mason Wheeler Communications, Inc.

This book would not exist without each of you.
Thank you.

Dedicated to
The Mentors of Scottsdale Bible Church

Table of Contents

A Word of Direction

Titus 2:4 declares, "Then they [the older women] can train the younger women to love their husbands and children, to be self-controlled and pure, to be busy at home, to be kind, and to be subject to their husbands, so that no one will malign the word of God" (NIV). After many fulfilling years as a young wife and mother, I now find myself at that stage in life when I qualify as one of those "older women" called to train (or mentor) the younger women. If you too are at that place, rejoice! It is a privilege—and an exciting one, at that—to be able to train and mentor a younger woman.

Since you have picked up this book, I assume you are interested in developing more meaningful relationships with other women of God. What better way to do it than to give away what you have received in your own journey as a woman of God? If that is your desire, I say thank you. Thank you for caring about connecting with and mentoring others. May the Father bless you for your desire and commitment.

I have attempted to keep the information in this book simple and succinct so that you are able to add your life imprint to each session. Your willingness to pass your life perspective to a younger woman can change the course of her life. As you do so, don't hold back from sharing your own failures or times of desperation, as well as the times in your life that have been filled with celebration.

This book is designed so that you can choose either to work your way straight through, from front to back, or pick sessions as they seem appropriate and relevant. With this in mind, choose a topic for each time you are to meet with your young friend and follow the format for that session in your preparation time as well as in the time you spend with your "daughter-of-the-heart." You will find it helpful also to record comments and ideas that emerge from your sharing times. Your genuine interest in her input will encourage a sense of significance in the heart of the young woman to whom you have committed yourself.

Reading through the book, you will find references to other materials that will expand your understanding and illumine your thoughts. I especially encourage you to pick up a copy of my companion book, *Between Women of God,* and also *The Stay-At-Home Mom* (revised and expanded edition, 1997), another one of my books, both published by Harvest House, to read in conjunction with this book. When other books are mentioned that might be helpful to you, you can turn to a supplemental reading list at the end of the book to find the name of the author and the publisher of the book so that you can more easily locate any of the additional resources in which you are interested.

This book is a multipurpose tool that can be used as:

    ⚘ a guide for meeting with a younger woman
    ⚘ a study guide for a small group
    ⚘ a personal study guide.

If you would like to begin a mentoring program that would include numerous women, please refer to the information on Mentors for Mothers at the end of this book. It is my prayer that God will use this material to encourage you and your daughter-of-the-heart and to take you both on to maturity in Christ!

Looking up,

Donna Otto

Donna Otto
Scottsdale, Arizona

Let's Talk About
the Character of a Christian

Getting Ready

Plan

Each week, remember to confirm with your young friend the time and location of your session together. Remember too that every time you have contact you will encourage her. For starters, you might suggest that she read Psalm 15, the "Christian Constitution."

Prepare

Read Psalm 15

Read and meditate on this Scripture. This would be a perfect lesson to use your dictionary and write down the multiple definitions for the word "character." In addition, if you have any books of famous quotes, you might like to use a few of them for your session. Here is one by Oswald Chambers to start with: "My worth to God in public is what I am in private."

Pray

Lord, help me to see the difference between being a Christian and having character. As a woman who desires to please God, may I be willing to forego the easy side of the street and step onto higher ground where standing tall for Christ is demanded.

Be Practical

In our society, the word "character" has been used so often it seems to have lost its punch. Keep your eyes and ears peeled for news reports about political campaigns being helped or hindered by character issues.

Our Time Together

Warm Up

To begin today's session, ask your young friend to describe in her own words her concept of *character.*

Sharing Your Thoughts

In a society where individual rights have reached gargantuan proportions, to be a woman with character means understanding your role as a servant.

Becoming a Christian does not automatically give you character any more than living in a garage would make you a car. Character is a tool to keep you from falling into the traps of the enemy, and the power behind that tool is your faith in Jesus.

Consider the difference between character and reputation. Abraham Lincoln said, "Character is like a tree and reputation like its shadow. The shadow is what we think of it, the tree is the real thing."

Here is an easy way to remember the difference:

- Reputation is who people think you are.
- Character is who you really are.

Only you and God know the difference.

Questions to Ponder

1. When you were a child, was character an important issue in your home?

2. Does character impact your work? Would you hire an extremely qualified employee who had less than a sterling character?

3. Does it take courage to have character? Does it take discpline? Explain your answers.

4. In your opinion, does it take suffering and pain to build character in a person?

5. Share about a time when you were affected by someone's reputation.

Praying for Each Other

As you join hands and pray together today, ask God to show you areas in your character that need refining. Be willing to take the steps necessary to participate in God's plan for improving your character.

Growing Together

1. Select another topic. It may be wise to piggyback on this topic to reinforce your time together today. Check for any assignments in the lesson you plan to work on.

2. Confirm the time and place of your next meeting.

3. Decide if you want to make a commitment to attempt change during the time between now and your next session. If you do, make sure the area is addressed clearly. Consider reading Psalm 15 daily until you meet again.

4. Pray together as you end your meeting. Continue to nurture your relationship with this young woman. Help her to see that you truly care about her and her loved ones. Hold hands, give her good eye contact, and connect with her heart. God will honor your efforts.

❧ Mentoring Moment ❧

"Character is what you are in the dark."
— DWIGHT L. MOODY

Let's Talk About Taming the Tongue

Getting Ready

Plan

Establish plans for your next session, making certain
you are in agreement about time and place. Suggest your young
friend read some or all of the Scripture verses below. This is a
transforming topic, and there are scores of relevant passages in
addition to the ones listed. If time permits, offer more verses.

Prepare

Read Job 19:2; Psalm 19:2,3; Ephesians 4:25; Colossians 3:9;
Proverbs 5:3,4; 16:27; 26:7; 29:20; Ecclesiastes 3:7b; 2 Timothy 2:16;
James 3:5-12; 2 Timothy 2:16

Review in your mind and heart any sermons, books, or
quotes on the topic of the tongue, gossip, or talking. This issue
is a challenge for everyone, so be prepared to dig in and
discover how it has influenced your young partner.

Pray

Dear Jesus, it is impossible to tame my tongue (see James
3:8) apart from Your power. I acknowledge the difficulty I have
experienced because I did not keep a guard over my mouth.
Please help me to assist this young woman in understanding
how to control her words.

Be Practical

Be prepared to talk about words and the tone of your voice.
Words are a product of the condition of our hearts, and the
tongue controls the entire body. Discuss those you each talk to
daily: children, Jesus, phone callers, mates, etc.

Our Time Together

Warm Up

Review your topic from last session. Ask your friend to share anything God did to affirm the topic in her heart.

As you move into this week's material, begin by finding out what words have been spoken to her that she holds in her heart. Were they hurtful? Helpful? Who spoke them? When?

Sharing Your Thoughts

The key concepts here are telling the truth and learning to listen.

When we speak, we must tell others and ourselves the truth. For instance, an abortion is just that, not an end to an unwanted pregnancy. If you are mad, admit you are mad and don't say, "Oh, I am just upset!" When asked to help with a project, be truthful . . . let your *yes* be *yes* and your *no* be *no*. Be honest in what you say.

Listening is an art that is more difficult for some to master than for others. Be quick to listen to God and others; be slow to speak. We tend to speak hastily and defensively when God instructs us and we don't want to hear it.

Questions to Ponder

1. Have you struggled with the issue of talking too much? Too little?

2. Do you use silence or chatter to manipulate, to keep someone at a distance, or to keep her from talking so you don't have to listen?

3. Is what you say okay, but how you say it needs some work?

4. Does what you say have any connection to what you read, watch, and listen to?

Praying for Each Other

During this season of prayer, make a time for silence. Ask God to remind you of any word spoken against another that needs forgiveness. Following silence and confession, ask God to correct your heart and its hurts so kindness will flow from your lips. Also include a time of listening for God's direction in your lives.

Growing Together

1. Have you chosen your next topic? If not, do so before you conclude this session, checking for any assignments and establishing your next meeting place and time.

2. Decide if you want to commit to any specific action regarding the tongue. If so, hold each other accountable to accomplish that commitment while you are apart. Consider memorizing the following twelve verses, which are only a few of the many that deal with the tongue. By memorizing them you will be building a "Scriptural guard" to check your words before you say them.

TWELVE TONGUE TAMERS

Check when memorized:

❑ "He who guards his lips guards his life, but he who speaks rashly will come to ruin" (Proverbs 13:3 NIV).

❑ "Do you see a man who speaks in haste? There is more hope for a fool than for him" (Proverbs 29:20 NIV).

❑ "He who answers before listening—that is his folly and his shame" (Proverbs 18:13 NIV).

❑ "But I tell you that men will have to give account on the day of judgment for every careless word they have spoken" (Matthew 12:36 NIV).

❑ "Do not let any unwholesome talk come out of your mouths, but only what is helpful for building others up according to their needs, that it may benefit those who listen" (Ephesians 4:29 NIV).

❑ "A man finds joy in giving an apt reply—and how good is a timely word!" (Proverbs 15:23 NIV).

- ❑ "He who guards his mouth and his tongue keeps himself from calamity" (Proverbs 21:23 NIV).

- ❑ A gentle answer turns away wrath, but a harsh word stirs up anger. . . . The tongue that brings healing is a tree of life, but a deceitful tongue crushes the spirit" (Proverbs 15:1,4 NIV).

- ❑ "Even a fool is thought wise if he keeps silent, and discerning if he holds his tongue" (Proverbs 17:28 NIV).

- ❑ "The words of a gossip are like choice morsels; they go down to a man's inmost parts" (Proverbs 18:8 NIV).

- ❑ "For 'Whosoever would love life and see good days must keep his tongue from evil and his lips from deceitful speech'" (1 Peter 3:10 NIV).

- ❑ "If anyone considers himself religious and yet does not keep a tight rein on his tongue, he deceives himself and his religion is worthless" (James 1:26 NIV).

3. Pray together. The helpfulness of kind words, gracious suggestions, and wise counsel should be acknowledged and praise offered to Him for these gifts. The hurt that happens and is harbored in our hearts also needs to be acknowledged. Each hurt should be offered to Him for healing. "If it is possible, as far as it depends on you, live at peace with everyone" (Romans 12:18 NIV).

❧ Mentoring Moment ❧

"Then you should say what you mean," the March Hare went on.
"I do," Alice hastily replied; "at least … at least I mean what I say and that's the same thing you know."
"Not the same thing a bit," said the Hatter.
— ALICE IN WONDERLAND

Let's Talk About Reasons to Stay Home

Getting Ready

Plan

Continue to contact your younger friend prior to your meeting confirming time, location, and topic. Ask her to be prepared to discuss her decision about having children and then why she chose to work or stay at home, whichever applies.

Prepare

Read Titus 2:3-5; Proverbs 31:27,28; Matthew 6:33. Read chapters 1 and 2 of The Stay-At-Home Mom *(Donna Otto, Harvest House).*

Read and meditate on the materials listed above. Consider these aspects of a career outside of the home: your own preference, the pressure of popular culture, financial needs, and/or the wishes of your husband.

Pray

Father God, do I have a bias on this subject? Am I able to assist this young woman in making a decision that would please You? If I made a poor decision as a young mother, have I asked forgiveness? Make me willing to be honest before this young woman.

Be Practical

This session will provide opportunities to talk about money, including how to make money at home, if necessary, and how to save money. Many statistics (which can be found throughout my book *The Stay-At-Home Mom*) confirm the difference in a child's attitudes and actions when he is being raised full-time by his mother at home. Don't hesitate to speak directly.

Our Time Together

Warm Up

Review the topic from your last session. If your young partner made a commitment to a specific action, be sure to ask her how she's doing. Clarify any areas of confusion.

To set the stage for today's topic, ask if her mother was a stay-at-home mom. If so, what did she most enjoy or remember about her mother? If not, what was hard about not having her mother available?

Sharing Your Thoughts

Here are the three main ideas: 1) Being home full-time encourages your faith to grow; 2) You are the best choice to parent; 3) The facts are in.

When we are home and needing to declare our dependence daily, we see God work. He sends finances and food and everything we need. Our faith grows, and we are able to show our children that God is trustworthy.

Daily you can see the impact of your decision on your children. No one can make decisions and choices for your child as well as you can. Children need their mothers. In 1992 more than 14 million women were home full-time with their children. In 1990, 1991, and 1993, the percentage of women in the work force declined for the first time since 1948.

The facts indicate that children grow to be more productive and useful if a mother's hand guides and directs as the primary caregiver.

Questions to Ponder

1. Have you considered why you want to stay at home or go to work?

2. Are finances the major consideration when you face staying home?

3. Are you able to believe that God has given you the responsibility to raise your children but that they still belong to Him?

4. Do you and your mate agree on the issue of staying at home?

5. If you are a single mother, can you still stay at home?

6. Do you have a hard time experiencing contentment?

Praying for Each Other

Confide in each other about longings of your heart. If you have had an expensive education and a fulfilling career, be grateful for these gifts and offer them to God as tools to raise children for Him.

Growing Together

1. Look at the session you will go over next week as you establish your meeting time and location. If there is an assignment, make sure the assignment is understood. Alter the task if necessary.

2. Decide if you want to commit to any specific act between now and your next session. Example: Each day I will hunt for circumstances through which I see God enlarging my faith.

3. Pray together. No matter how difficult or easy this topic is for you and your young friend, you will need to encourage her to be steadfast. Raising children is a twenty-year investment. The choice to stay at home is sometimes ridiculed. Ask God to grant comfort and assurance in the choice to be a stay-at-home mom.

Mentoring Moment

WET OATMEAL KISSES

The baby is teething. The children are fighting.
Your husband just called and said, "Eat dinner without me."
One of these days you'll explode and shout to the kids,
"Why don't you grow up and act your age?"
And they will.

Or, "You guys get outside and find yourselves something to do.
And don't slam the door!" And they don't.
You'll straighten their bedrooms all neat and tidy,
toys displayed on the shelf, hangers
in the closet, animals caged. You'll yell,
"Now I want it to stay this way!"
And it will.

You will prepare a perfect dinner with a salad
that hasn't had all the olives picked out and a cake
with no finger traces in the icing and you'll say,
"Now THIS is a meal for company."
And you will eat it alone.

You'll yell, "I want complete privacy on the phone.
No screaming. Do you hear me?" And no one will answer.
No more plastic tablecloths stained with spaghetti.
No more dandelion bouquets. No more iron-on patches.
No more wet, knotted shoelaces,
muddy boots or rubber bands for ponytails.

Imagine. A lipstick with a point. No babysitter for New Year's Eve,
washing clothes only once a week, no PTA meetings or silly school plays
where your child is a tree. No carpools,
blaring stereos or forgotten lunch money.

No more Christmas presents made of library paste and toothpicks.
No more wet oatmeal kisses. No more tooth fairy.
No more giggles in the dark, scraped knees
to kiss or sticky fingers to clean.
Only a voice asking: "Why don't you grow up?"

And the silence echoes: "I did."

— ANONYMOUS

Let's Talk About Disciplines of a Godly Woman

Getting Ready

Plan

Once again make certain that your schedules are coordinated for the time and location of your next meeting. Think of this session as one that can head in several directions: a call to Christ, a deeper commitment as a woman of God, or perhaps facing and dealing seriously with sin.

Prepare

Read Romans 12:1,2; John 10:10; 1 Samuel 16:7; Galatians 5:22,23; 2 Corinthians 4:16,17; Romans 9:20,21

Read and meditate on the Scriptures listed above. Feel free to add more as you feel inclined. Determine as best you can which direction your young partner most needs to go, and prepare your heart to head in that direction. If you are not certain of her decision for Christ, you may want to have additional material available. I would suggest the *Four Spiritual Laws* booklet produced by Campus Crusade. You might also prepare to do a word study on "discipline," and evaluate how our society deals with discipline.

Pray

Father, help me to return in memory to the day I found You in my heart. Do I still have my "first love"? Help me to assist this young woman to seek Your face. Be the Leader in our discussion, and help us both to desire to be godly.

Be Practical

This may be a reality-check session. Often we want to achieve something without the discipline required to do so. If discipline is lacking in one area, usually it is lacking in other areas as well. Develop this topic and look for ways to help create discipline in your lives.

Our Time Together

Warm Up

Review the topic from last session. If follow-up is indicated, take the time now. Don't feel obligated to do a new topic today in lieu of further exploring or finishing the prior topic. Our aim is for growth and deepening, so stay with whatever topic is necessary until you feel it has served its purpose.

Sharing Your Thoughts

As suggested earlier, if you are uncertain of your young partner's relationship with Christ, be sure you start this session with an opportunity to make Jesus first in her world. Beyond this step, make sure these concepts are understood: acceptance of self as God made her, recognition of God's deep love for her, acknowledgment that God is good and so is everything He does. From this framework, you can approach any or all of the following:

Bible Study	Prayer	Service
Giftedness	Abilities	Attitudes
Being vs. Doing	Fruit of the Spirit	God's Will

Questions to Ponder

1. What keeps you from consistency in your spiritual growth?

2. Discuss the areas in your life that demonstrate a lack of discipline.

3. Look at the topics listed under "Sharing Your Thoughts." Which of these would you begin expending energy on immediately?

4. Is Jesus your first love? Do you sense that He is relegated to a place lower than first place?

5. How does the world squeeze you into its mold for living each day? How would you like to change that?

Praying for Each Other

Now is a great time to make this statement: "I have not arrived ... but I am surviving." Seek to be honest in your prayer time. Freely confess the need for more of God in your world. We can never achieve godliness; rather we become more godly as we draw closer to God.

Growing Together

1. Choose a topic for your next session, and check for any advance assignments.

2. Check your calendars for the time and place of your next meeting.

3. Again, this lesson really calls for some specific action. Take the time to assess that action and make a commitment to each other. It may be as simple as choosing to show more love to others or as intense as giving up a lifelong habit that separates you from God.

4. Pray together. Touch your daughter-of-the-heart's hand or arm as you prepare to pray together. If this session has helped your young friend to recognize a need, this prayer time could be a turning point, a change point in her life. Don't rush—let the Holy Spirit do His job in both of your hearts.

❧ Mentoring Moment ❧

"It is good to do the work of God ...
better still to do His will."

— AUTHOR UNKNOWN

Let's Talk About
Fashioning Your Mental Wardrobe

Getting Ready
Plan
Establishing regular patterns for your meeting times and places may provide you with an opportunity to help your young friend develop her organizational skills. Show her how to track appointments and tasks in a notebook or calendar.

Prepare
Read Deuteronomy 6:6-10; Colossians 3:12-17; Psalm 24:4; Psalm 101:3

Read and meditate on the assigned Scripture passages. You may find it helpful to consult a dictionary for a definition of "purity." Find examples from current magazines, TV shows, and films to demonstrate the difficulty of maintaining a pure life in our society.

Pray
Lord, I want to be pure as You are pure. Have I allowed unwholesome actions, images, or thoughts to dwell in me? Help me rely on Your promptings toward holiness as I seek to grow in You.

Be Practical
Practice answering the question "What shall I wear today?" with principles from the Colossians passage listed above. Browse through a fashion magazine and have some fun exploring styles, colors, wardrobe planning, and even closet cleaning! Then consider issues of appropriateness and motivation.

Our Time Together

Warm Up

Review the last topic covered and follow up any unresolved issues or concerns. Look for that "sigh" of understanding.

Sharing Your Thoughts

Much like we clothe our bodies, we clothe our minds. What shall we put on mentally today? Biblical thinking!

Currently popular "politically correct" thinking allows for no absolutes, focuses solely on the right of the individual, and scoffs at the idea of dying to self and living for God's glory. These attitudes have even invaded some churches, resulting in Christians who confuse someone's well-meaning agenda with what God actually says.

Lead your young friend to understand the importance of deliberately putting on biblical thinking every hour of every day. No more wondering what to wear!

Questions to Ponder

1. How much time do you spend on your wardrobe? Don't forget to include shopping, washing, ironing, dressing, and experimenting with new looks.

2. Do you spend as much time developing your mental wardrobe?

3. If not, why not? If the concept of "mental dressing" is new to you, give yourself time to absorb and implement this new challenge.

4. Have you developed thought patterns that may need to be revised? If so, search for relevant topics in the Scriptures to gain God's perspective on your thoughts.

5. Consider the important people in your life. How does their thinking affect you? Are you allowing their thoughts to direct yours?

Praying for Each Other

Ask God to help you see your thought patterns as He does and to free you from feeling fearful about giving up ways of thinking that have become comfortable over the years. We want to have the mind of Christ and to wear apparel that separates us from the world's thinking.

Growing Together

1. Choose your next topic and any related assignments. Or, you may want to designate your next session as a review of previous sessions. If so, prepare to share how the Lord is growing you closer to Him and to each other.

2. Select a time and location for your next session. Be creative: Celebrate spring weather by meeting on a park bench, or enjoy winter in front of a cozy fireplace.

3. Consider challenging each other to memorize the Colossians passage to help you think about your mental wardrobe at least as often as you think about your fashion wardrobe.

4. Pray together. Ask God to help you avoid being too preoccupied with or not concerned enough about your outer appearance. Seek a balance that will please Him.

❧ Mentoring Moment ❧

"Your beauty should not come from outward adornment, such as braided hair and the wearing of gold jewelry and fine clothes. Instead, it should be that of your inner self, the unfading beauty of a gentle and quiet spirit, which is of great worth in God's sight."

— 1 Peter 3:3,4 (NIV)

"The spirit of the age seeps into the church."

— FRANCIS SCHAEFFER

Let's Talk About Being Imitators

Getting Ready

Plan

Make sure that enough time has been scheduled to cover this lesson.

Prepare

Read 1 Thessalonians 1:6,7; 2:14; Hebrews 6:12; 13:7; 2 Thessalonians 3:7; Colossians 3:10; 3 John 11; Ephesians 5:1

Read and meditate on the assigned Scriptures. Find a dictionary definition for the word "imitation." Consider the implications of being a follower in relation to the way an actor mimics.

Pray

Father, please show me the people and things I have tended to imitate in the past. Have I felt compelled to follow the crowd? Whom do I desire to imitate now?

Be Practical

Find examples of famous personalities and performers who are currently being mimicked. Perhaps it's a hairstyle, a fitness program, or an attitude that is being copied across the country. Remember when hula hoops were all the rage? Remember when one commercial sparked the popular rude response, "Not!"?

Our Time Together

Warm Up

Play a round of "Simon Says" to set the tone for a discussion of what it means to be a follower. Try to remember incidents from childhood or adolescence when you or your friends played "Simon Says" in real life.

Sharing Your Thoughts

Sometimes we are drawn to imitate a public figure for the wrong reasons. We find ourselves attracted by wealth, beauty, popularity, or personality, often overlooking more worthwhile qualities in someone who may be far from the spotlight. Seek to see the value in choosing the best person to imitate. The next best thing to being wise oneself is to live in a circle of those who are.

Questions to Ponder

1. What does it mean to be a follower?

2. Upon reflection, did you discover that you have been imitating someone without realizing it? Who and why?

3. When choosing someone to follow, should character or performance be the primary consideration?

4. What does the Bible say about being "followers of Christ"?

5. Can you see why it is less desirable to follow a person than to follow the Christ you see in that person? Explain.

Praying for Each Other

Ask God to reveal areas where you may be following unwisely. Make a commitment to seek Him and His people. Ask Him to provide wisdom to discern positive mentors for you to imitate.

Growing Together

1. Select the topic for your next meeting, perhaps one that relates well to today's subject, and confirm the place and time of your next meeting.

2. This would be an excellent time to encourage your partner to reevaluate the relationships in her world. She may need extra

help if she has just recognized the dangers of an unhealthy relationship or unwise imitation.

3. Pray together. If the situation allows, you will find it meaningful to kneel together in humility before God while seeking sensitivity in the area of relationships that need to be changed. Let God direct your efforts for His holy purposes.

❧ Mentoring Moment ❧

The following hymn is not often sung today, but I am convinced that young men and women still yearn for the character traits expressed so well here. Today's young people are eagerly looking for models and mentors to follow in the ways of truth, purity, strength, and courage.

I WOULD BE TRUE

I would be true, for there are those who trust me;
I would be pure, for there are those who care.
I would be strong, for there is much to suffer;
I would be brave, for there is much to dare—
I would be brave, for there is much to dare.

I would be friend of all—the foe, the friendless;
I would be giving, and forget the gift.
I would be humble, for I know my weakness;
I would look up, and laugh, and love, and lift—
I would look up, and laugh, and love, and lift.

— HOWARD ARNOLD WALTER, 1917

Let's Talk About Unity

Getting Ready

Plan

Your weekly contact with your young friend is important to the building of your relationship. Take time to contact her and confirm your plans.

Prepare

Meditate on the book of Ephesians, especially chapter 4:1-6. Think about the concept of unity in your world.

Pray

Lord, help me to see the reasons why I am not unified with You and with Your family. If unforgiveness stands in the way of my being in unity with You, I desire to confess my sins and to be made right and whole.

Be Practical

Find a book or a magazine on gardening, or make a trip to the nursery near your home. Do your best to discover the concept of unity in the gardening field.

Warm Up

Look up the word *unified* in the dictionary together. Allow your daughter-of-the-heart to brainstorm her ideas and concepts about this very important topic as a member of the family of God.

Sharing Your Thoughts

I am a gardener of sorts. I grow both flowers and vegetables. Living in the sunny, warm, arid state of Arizona, the opportunity to garden most of the year is available to me. My experiences with gardening have been varied. Each experience brings me closer to understanding how, just like the plants in my gardens, we work together in unity.

In the book of Ephesians, Paul encourages the church to be in love with one another. He uses the word "love" nine times in the six chapters in this book, while he uses the word only 23 times in all of the other letters he writes. He tells his readers that there are no differences in Christ. There are not Jews and Gentiles, just fellow men and women in Christ.

There are seven elements of unity found in Ephesians 4:4-6. They are:

1. one body—the church of Jesus

2. one Spirit—the Holy Spirit

3. one hope—the future, which is the same for all of us

4. one Lord—the head of the church

5. one faith—the subjective faith which we exercise

6. one baptism—water or not, it refers to our identification with Christ

7. one God and Father—the relationship God has with all of us

We are growing together, planted together, planted with Him—experiencing with Him the understanding of His death for all.

One, not many. When I plant vegetables, they are vegetables—yes, a variety, but vegetables in one garden, with one gardener, one sun, and one water source. It's the same with mixed flower seeds. They are a combination of flowers in one package needing the gardener, water, and sun to help them grow.

We are united by the act of the cross. Those outside of the family of God are able to see the work of the cross in our lives by the unity we live. Stay connected to Jesus and to one another at all costs. Our differences are expected; they make us interesting to talk to but should never separate us from one another.

Questions to Ponder

1. Do you regularly find discord with certain individuals or certain personality types? If so, why?

2. As a child did you see unity lived out in your family? In your church?

3. What is the closest group of people you have ever been a part of? What made it so close?

4. What does it take for you to personally feel a sense of unity with other believers?

5. Describe a time when you were left out.

Praying for Each Other

As you pray together, hold hands and draw as close to one another as possible. This will give a sense of unity. This prayer time would be a good time to ask one another the question, "Are we okay with each other?" If not, you can talk it out together. If all is well, you can thank God for the unity you share and enjoy.

Growing Together

1. Continue to look forward to your next session. Appoint a time, location, and topic that is agreeable to both of you. Check the session you have chosen for any assignments.

2. This week agree to evaluate relationships each of you have with family and friends. Are these relationships demonstrating unity? Plan to follow up on this topic during your next time together.

3. Continue to share prayer requests with one another.

❀ Mentoring Moment ❀

In an illustration from an *Upwords* newsletter written by Max Lucado, the introduction finds all believers on one ship with One Captain and One Destination. There is disharmony among the crew because they don't look alike or sound alike, nor are they interested in the same actions on board.

LIFE ABOARD THE FELLOW-SHIP
by Max Lucado

"The variety of dress is not nearly as disturbing as the plethora of opinions. Some think once you're on the boat you can't get off. Others say it'd be foolish to go overboard, but the choice is yours. Some believe you volunteer for service, others believe you were destined to be here before the ship was even built. Some feel a storm of great tribulation will strike before we dock, others say it won't hit until we are safely ashore. There are those who think the officers should wear robes, there are those who think there should be no officers at all, and there are those who think we are all officers and should all wear robes. And then there is the weekly meeting at which the Captain is thanked and his words are read. All agree on its importance, but few agree on its nature. Some want it loud, others quiet. Some want ritual, others spontaneity."

Lucado ends this portion with Ephesians 4:3:

"Make every effort to keep the unity of the Spirit through the bond of peace."

Let's Talk About Knowing and Finding His Purpose

Getting Ready

Plan

Before your next meeting, call your young friend to confirm the location, time, and topic, and ask her to be prepared to share a decision she has made. In the process of this decision, what tools did she use to find God's will?

Prepare

Read Matthew 21:37-30; Acts 5:29; Colossians 3 and 4:2-4; Titus 2:3-5; Hebrews 11:8; 1 Peter 1:2

Meditate on these passages as well as others that provide you with instructions and with His desire for obedience in our lives.

Pray

Lord, I have seen Your purpose and will in my life through carefully studying and following Your Word. The way of God is the direction found in the Scriptures. May I find the words to encourage my daughter-of-the-heart to seek Your will and obey it daily.

Be Practical

This could be a session on how to make decisions. Each of us makes decisions on a daily basis. Each decision influences us much more than we imagine. Consider the following daily decisions and their ramifications:

- the time you get up
- what you eat
- the way you drive to work
- how you speak to your family and friends
- how you spend your time

Take these daily, simple concepts, and as many others as time permits, and find an answer or two from the Scriptures.

Warm Up

As you begin your time together, ask her the questions you have asked and answered this week. Review the simple, practical decisions you make daily, and use these points as a place to jump into the discussion on finding and knowing God's will.

Sharing Your Thoughts

Every day Christians ask, "What is God's will for my life?" The question is often followed by, "How do I find God's will?" or "How do I know if it is God's will?"

Perhaps you are like me. I'd like Jesus to write me a book of my own, and each chapter would represent a decade of my life, and each paragraph would tell me how to live each year within that decade. The reality is that there are no books named Donna in the Bible, but they all have my name written in them.

To know His will is to know Him. To study His Word and obey His commands is to know Him. If you are already. . .

- committed to Christ as Lord of your life
- reading His Word
- listening to His Holy Spirit
- praying
- witnessing
- fellowshipping with other believers
- knowing and using your spiritual gifts
- studying His Word
- meditating
- serving others

. . . then your ability to know Him and listen to Him is already in place. When you make a decision, you know the Word well enough to know that whatever you are deciding is not in conflict with His instructions. Each portion of your decision is found in knowing God. If you know God, you will know His will.

Elisabeth Elliot reduces making decisions and knowing God's will to the ability to trust and obey. If you know, you can trust. If you trust, you will obey.

Questions to Ponder

1. What was the hardest decision you ever made? Why?

2. What was the best decision you made? Why? How did you make that choice?

3. Reflect and discuss a time when you made a bad decision. Talk through the process, the decision, and the results.

4. What, regarding God's will in your life, are you certain about?

5. List two to five specific things that you are certain are God's will. Example: It is God's will that all men should know Him.

Praying for Each Other

Make the time, as well as the prayer, a time of unraveling what you know about God and His Word. We can accept information as truth and discover later it is not truth. Ask God to reveal any pieces of information that may not be truth.

Growing Together

1. Once again establish your next meeting time, location, and topic. Check the lesson you are selecting for any assignments.

2. Ask your young friend if she has a decision pending for which she is searching for God's answer and direction. If so, use this as a teaching tool to help her align her thinking with God's.

3. Pray over each of the topics you have discussed today.

❦ Mentoring Moment ❦

"I am approached with the most opposite opinions and advice, and that by religious men who are equally certain that they represent the Divine Will. I am sure that either the one or the other class is mistaken in that belief, and perhaps, in some respect, both. I hope it will not be irreverent for me to say that if it is probable that God would reveal His will to others on a point so connected with my duty, it might be supposed that He would reveal it directly to me; for unless I am more deceived in myself than I often am, it is my earnest desire to know the will of Providence in this matter. And if I can learn what it is, I will do it. These are not, however, the days of miracles, and I suppose it will be granted that I am not to expect a direct revelation. I must study the plain physical facts of the case, ascertain what is possible, and learn what appears to be wise and right. The subject is difficult, and good men do not agree."

—ABRAHAM LINCOLN
(on the topic of slavery)

Let's Talk About Busyness

Getting Ready
Plan
Call your young friend and confirm your session. Ask her to consider areas of her life where she feels too busy and be prepared to talk about those areas. Additionally, ask her to keep a log of her activities for the next seven days. (You may want to provide her a prepared sheet that will allow her to just fill in the blanks.)

Prepare
If you have these books, scan their information: My book *Get More Done in Less Time; Tyranny of the Urgent* by Charles Hummel; *Ordering Your Private World* by Gordon McDonald; *Discipline, the Glad Surrender* by Elisabeth Elliot; *Celebration of Discipline* (chapter on solitude) by Richard Foster.

Pray
Dear Jesus, help me to clear my thoughts and rearrange my own priorities, allowing me to see how I use my time. Also, give me the ability to see why I hurry, hurry, hurry. Finally, may I be willing to rearrange my life to make it less busy.

Be Practical
Make a log of your own week. Decide what you would like to readjust. Anne Ortlund encourages women to reevaluate their schedules regularly every five years to take a serious look at not only schedules and priorities, but belief systems. These exercises

will help you know where you spend your time and how you want to spend your time. If there is a conflict, you can begin to adjust. This tool is used by many CEOs throughout America.

Warm Up

This is the time to go over your daily log for the past week. If you did not do a log, think about why you didn't, and then try to recall, in one-hour increments, how you spent each day.

Sharing Your Thoughts

A friend sent me a Cathy card that said, "I'm too busy to call. I'm too busy to visit. I'm too busy to write a letter." As you open the card you see Cathy with her best grin standing in front of a greeting card display case. She is holding a few cards and has a few more at her feet. The caption reads, "However, I've managed to find seven hours to stand around reading all the greeting cards." The humor of the card is outweighed by the ring of truth. We always have time to do what we want to do.

How does this busyness creep into our lives? Here are a few possibilities:

- We think busyness is good or godly.
- Busyness makes us look important.
- Busyness makes us feel important.
- Modern conveniences give us more time.
- We can't decide.
- We say yes more than no, or just don't know when to say which.
- Busyness is progress.
- Everyone is busy, so just "buck up."
- Our culture is busy, and we must keep up.

To counteract this way of busyness we must make time for quiet solitude and restoration. Making time for quiet is essential if we are to hear from God about the direction of our lives. If we are too busy to pray and find quiet before the God of the Universe—the Lord of our lives—we are TOO busy.

Questions to Ponder

1. Do you say "hurry up" to your children? How often?

2. Do you exceed the speed limit to get places on time? How often?

3. Is dinner hour just a few minutes? Do you eat in the car?

4. Does your life have quiet time? How often? By accident or by schedule?

5. Describe how you feel when you are rushing, rushing, rushing.

Praying for Each Other

Take time today for a longer session of prayer. Help each other quiet your hearts and minds long enough to sense rest and peacefulness. Be willing to heed what you hear from this time of prayer and quiet. Perhaps you could change your location for this time of prayer. If there is a garden near your meeting location, you might consider going there for prayer.

Growing Together

1. Once again establish your next topic, location, time, and assignments. Repeat, Repeat, Repeat. It is one way we learn.

2. The possibilities for accountability and assistance to one another as a result of this session are many. Consider these suggestions:

   • Rise early and phone each other one day this week.

   • If your young friend has children, you might offer to watch the children while she has a quiet session.

   • Perhaps an extra time together just for more prayer and quiet would work in your schedule.

   • Hold each other accountable for a ten-minute-per-day time of solitude.

   • Encourage each other to cut out or slow down in one area of your lives.

   • Use your imagination about other ways to cut back on busyness.

3. Continue to pray for this dear daughter-of-the-heart whom God has sent for you to watch over her soul.

Mentoring Moment

TWENTY-THIRD PSALM FOR BUSY PEOPLE

The Lord is my pacesetter, I shall not rush during the day.
He makes me stop for quiet intervals, to plan my life.
He provides me with images of stillness, which restore my serenity in the rush.
He leads me in ways of efficiency through calmness of mind in doing tasks wisely.
And His guidance is peace in choosing the proper tasks.
Even though I have many things to accomplish each day, I will not fret, for His presence is here.
His timelessness, His all-importance will keep me in balance.
He prepares refreshment and renewal in the midst of my activity with a quiet time.
By anointing my mind with His oils of tranquillity,
My cup of joyous energy overflows as I charge ahead!
Surely, harmony and reflectiveness shall be the fruit of my hours,
For I shall walk in the path of my Lord and dwell in His house forever, being ever grateful for His love and salvation.

—AUTHOR UNKNOWN

Let's Talk About Trying Trust

Getting Ready

Plan
It seems unnecessary to confirm the time, location, and topic each week, but we are all prone to forget and make mistakes. This weekly contact provides a helpful nudge as well as one more opportunity to say hello. Suggest to your young friend that she read the first two chapters of Job this week.

Prepare
Read as much of the book of Job as possible, but especially the first two chapters and Job 13:15. The topic of trust can be linked to adversity or prosperity. Job trusted through times of prosperity and adversity. His life is a great model.

Pray
Lord, help me to understand this concept of trust in a deep way. I desire to trust You in all things, not just in the situations I choose. May I understand Your sufficiency, which will cause me to trust You more.

Be Practical
Make a list of ways we choose to trust people. Take time with this list. You will be amazed how many times we choose to trust others in our day-to-day activities. Example: We trust the Department of Transportation as it establishes the stop signs, red lights, and speed limits in our city.

Warm Up

Go over your list of "trusts" with your young friend. Give her opportunities to add to your list. This will set the stage for acknowledging the ability to trust and move closer to trusting God as Job did.

Sharing Your Thoughts

This amazing story of the life of Job is very powerful. Job is one of the oldest (perhaps *the* oldest) and longest books of the Bible. Many scholars believe it was likely written by Job. While many find the story sad or discouraging, I find it very stimulating. Job has grown and seems to fully understand and live out the New Testament principle of "I am the vine; you are the branches. If a man remains in me and I in him, he will bear much fruit; apart from me you can do nothing" (John 15:5).

While this book has 42 chapters, like a good author, the writer gets right to the heart of the message by describing Job three different ways in the first 25 verses. He is "blameless, upright and fearing God." Job speaks nine of the most powerful words ever written: "Though he slay me, yet will I hope [trust] in him."

Job's character is blameless. Job acknowledges that all of his belongings come from God and belong to God. Job attests that he himself came naked into the world and will leave the same way, proudly proclaiming that apart from God he is nothing.

Suddenly this wealthy, prominent man is attacked. Satan does the attacking with God's permission. The attacks have only one boundary—Satan can take family, health, and possessions, but not Job's life. Yet, after being attacked on all of these fronts, Job still trusts. Job understands two significant traits of trust:

1. God, the object of his trust, is trustworthy.

2. Trust is a choice.

Questions to Ponder

1. Discuss the attributes of God.

2. Try to discover why trusting is personally hard. Often life experiences sabotage our trust levels.

3. Who do you trust most on this earth? Why?

4. What would you be able to lay down before God to demonstrate your trust?

Praying for Each Other

The topic of trust is essential to our walk of faith. To allow God to be the Lord of our lives and submit all to Him is not easy, but it is what God desires from us and has enabled us to accomplish as we walk on earth.

Growing Together

1. As you finish this session you will need to prepare for the next topic, location, and time. You may have decided on the same time and place each week, but it is still important to reiterate this information.

2. As you leave one another, select one specific area in your lives to trust in the Lord until you meet again. You may want to memorize Proverbs 3:5-6:

   > Trust in the Lord with all your heart and lean not on your own understanding; in all your ways acknowledge him, and he will make your paths straight.

3. Continue to nurture the relationship with your young friend. Make her certain of your connection with her heart and mind. Let her know that you are praying for her and are available to her.

❧ Mentoring Moment ❧

"Though He slay me, yet will I trust Him" (Job 13:15 KJV).

"Though He slay me, I will hope in Him" (NASB).

"Though he slay me, yet will I hope in him" (NIV).

"God may kill me for saying this—in fact, I expect him to. Nevertheless I am going to argue my case with him" (TLB).

Let's Talk About Contentment—"At-One-Ment"

Getting Ready

Plan

You have already set the date and time for this session, but a gentle and loving reminder provides another contact as well as a reminder. Call your friend, jot her a note, or send her something and add a sticky tab about your meeting.

Prepare

Read Exodus 20; Luke 3:14; 2 Corinthians 12:10; Philippians 4:11; 1 Timothy 6:6-8; Hebrews 13:5

We all need reminders and reinforcements about this contentment. Meditate on these passages, as well as the book of Acts. If you have a copy of *Foxe's Book of Martyrs*, or any biography of a missionary, reread portions to refresh yourself with the sacrifice and determination of the early church.

Pray

Jesus, looking around I often see something I want or need. I desire to live in the world, but not be of the world. May I rejoice with those who have more than me. I desire to be content with what Your hand has given me.

Be Practical

Most Americans watch TV and read some newspapers or weekly periodicals. Take any one of those and make a list of what you are encouraged to own. In the course of a one-hour TV program or an evening of TV watching, make a list of how many items the merchants try to sell you. Do the same with just one magazine. It might be more interesting if you choose a magazine or TV show that is familiar to your young friend. Another idea is to get a small camping tent and set it up as a visual before your daughter-of-the-heart arrives or perhaps you might choose to set it up together. Ask her if she is content—well-tented. I have done this, and it is very memorable.

Warm Up

Take your research from the TV or magazine and examine the data together. Discuss how often we are subjected to bigger and better options. This would be a great time to share any personal insight you have regarding your own lack of contentment.

Sharing Your Thoughts

Paul's discussion of contentment found in Philippians sets the stage for this topic. He instructs us to be content no matter what we have. Whether we have much or we have little, we should be content. We should work at being well-tented, content in what we have.

This concept of contentment seems simple enough, and I suppose it is clear. The difficulty is working it into our lives. Man is made to enjoy what he sees, and our sin nature causes us to lust. To be satisfied, or to find sufficiency in where we live, how much we eat, what we drive, what we wear, where we go, who our friends are, what our church is, how much education we have, who our children, mates, and parents are, is not a simple task. Hebrews advises us to be content with such things as we have.

Going back to the Ten Commandments we find that we should not covet our neighbor's home, spouse, male or female servant (dishwasher or bread maker), ox or donkey (new car), or anything. The list seems complete. It seems the question is, *How do I get from not coveting to contentment?*

The answer is through at-one-ment with God. Acknowledge His abundance and ability to provide anything and everything. To be content is to be at-one with God and His decisions for your life, to trust Him for all His gifts and goodness to you. He has given you life and all the necessary accessories. Acceptance of God's plan in our lives is at the root of contentment and satisfaction. While it is true that God ordained that we participate with Him on our journey through life, He did not plan for us to be in charge. That is His task. When I start to covet something, anything, I have allowed myself to become my own god. When I do that, I break yet another of the Ten Commandments: "Thou shalt have no other God before me." It takes trust and practice to be content and at one with God.

Questions to Ponder

1. Do you find yourself comparing what you have and who you are with your friends and family members?

2. Do you think you are ambitious? If so, how could ambition cause you to be discontent?

3. Make a list of the things that cause you temptation.

4. Describe a time when you were grateful and glad for something or for an event that happened in your life.

5. Is contentment an issue in your world? How does it rank with other issues in your world?

Praying for Each Other

Join hands and pray for one another. Seek to be sensitive to what you have already discussed in this session as you ask for God's enablement to move you further into at-one-ment with Him. The ability to be content and satisfied with God's sufficiency is life-changing.

Growing Together

1. Determine when and where you will meet as you make your next topical selection.

2. This is an excellent session to set up some accountability with one another. Perhaps one of you reads too many catalogs, which causes dissatisfaction with what you own, or watches too many romance movies, which can cause dissatisfaction in marriage. After you have explored these areas, set up some kind of checks and balances.

3. Pray together. Ask God to cause the truths you have discussed to go deep into your heart.

❧ Mentoring Moment ❧

"It is a wise man who knows when he has enough. The effort to get more may result in misfortune and misery."

— UNKNOWN

Let's Talk About Serving

Getting Ready
Plan
Each week remember to confirm with your young friend the time and location of your next session together. Every contact with her will increase your ability to relate to one another.

Prepare
Read Exodus 24:13; 33:11; Matthew 22:37-40; 25:21

This lesson should bring you closer to the definition of the terms *servant, slave,* and *ministry.* As you search the passages listed above, you will also face the issue of how much love you and your young friend truly have for mankind. Read the Bible, looking for as many servants of God and man as you can find.

Pray
Lord, help me to assess in my own life how willing I am to serve anyone. May I be honest about the areas I am willing to give my time and attention to. As I evaluate these issues in my life, help me to bring fresh light into the heart of my young friend about her desire to serve, her need to serve, and the direction she should take.

Be Practical
Serving is not a popular topic in any of our lives. It might be useful to have some information about the need for volunteers in America. You might consider calling your local public school to find how many willing servants are in the classrooms. Gather

any data to illustrate how uncommon it is to find slaves or servants in the last decade of the twentieth century.

Warm Up

As you begin your time together, ask your daughter-of-the-heart two questions:

1. As best as she can remember, except for her parents, who has served her the most?

2. What is she currently doing that she would call service?

Sharing Your Thoughts

As women committed to making Christ Lord of our lives, serving is important. Once our decision for God is completed, our lives are not our own, and we begin to look for ways to please Him. One way we do this is by sharing our faith with others.

We also receive spiritual gifts at the time of our conversion, and these gifts belong to the family of God. Each believer has the joy of stewarding these gifts. Add to the spiritual gifts our natural talents and resources of time, energy, and finances, and we begin to see a plan of how we can best serve God and the family of God.

As we mature in our walk with God, we take on the fruit of knowing God in more intimate ways, and growth appears in areas such as kindness, humility, compassion, perseverance, and obedience. Often we begin to find specific opportunities to serve that challenge us.

Joshua was first a servant to Moses; it was actually his official title. Later he became known as the servant of Jehovah. Joshua handled many of the details for Moses. The Hebrew word used about Joshua in Exodus is very much like the Greek word that means "deacon." So Joshua served Moses as his deacon. Joshua loved Moses and God, and he learned about serving God by serving Moses. The lawyer in Matthew who asked what the greatest commandment was quickly found that loving God and one another were the two on which everything else is based. If I love, I will serve.

Our pastor has said for years, "We all want to be slaves/servants until someone treats us like one."

Questions to Ponder

1. How do you feel about being a servant?

2. As a child did you have regular opportunities to serve family, friends, and neighbors?

3. Do you see the servant as a strong individual or a weak individual?

4. What are your talents, spiritual gifts, and interests?

5. How could you use your talents, spiritual gifts, and interests to serve others?

Praying for Each Other

As you join in prayer over this tremendously important topic, look for ways to serve your young friend. Ask God to reveal anything that hinders the ability to love one another, and give yourself freely to serving one another.

Growing Together

1. Select your next topic. Look for any assignments in the next session and make certain your younger friend understands the assignment.

2. Set the date and location of your next meeting.

3. Discuss the possibility of serving together in some work of the Kingdom.

4. Encourage your friend to move forward. If, until now, she has never understood the need to serve one another by loving and looking for ways to minister, affirm her interest and invest in her desire to add serving to her life.

❧ Mentoring Moment ❧

"Had I but served my God with half the zeal
I serve my King, he would not in mine age
Have left me naked to mine enemies."
—SHAKESPEARE, *HENRY VIII*, III, 2

Let's Talk About the Way to Your Husband's Heart

Getting Ready

Plan

Confirm with an encouraging note or telephone call your time, location, and topic for this session.

Prepare

Read Romans 15:7; Ephesians 4:32; Psalm 24:3,4; Romans 12:18. Refer to the How to Love Your Husband *session on page 71. Review your husband's favorite recipes and menus.*

Read and meditate on the above Scriptures. Plan your husband's favorite dinner and add more of his favorite foods to next week's marketing list: popsicles, corn chips, canned peaches, ingredients for homemade cookies, or old-fashioned hot dogs like he gets at his favorite sports arena.

Pray

Father, do I find joy in serving the foods my husband likes? Do I think more often about ministering to his needs or manipulating him to meet my needs? Is there really acceptance in my heart for this man you sent to me, or is there just action without acceptance? Help me this week to speak straight from my heart about my relationship with my husband.

Be Practical

This would be a good session to teach your young friend some things about food: its preparation, presentation, or effect on people in our homes. Talk about fragrance or lighting or anything you do to create a special atmosphere for your loved ones.

Our Time Together

Warm Up

Review the topic from your last session and revisit any issues that need a little extra time. Don't be disappointed if your young friend does not want to revisit a topic because some topics will meet her needs more than others.

Sharing Your Thoughts

Having an attitude of acceptance toward your husband's preferences helps you keep short accounts with him. Be constantly aware of any need to offer and receive forgiveness. If he is a man unable or unwilling to ask for forgiveness, then remember to be at peace with him as much as is possible" (see Romans 12:18). You will be rewarded by the Father with a peaceful heart for accepting this husband that God has given, and in time you will be rewarded by your husband in his own way for finding ways to favor and serve him. This is not to say that you will always be able to serve your husband's favorite meal at the time he prefers and in a perfect atmosphere. But the ability to serve without resentment or pressure is a great gift to your marriage.

Questions to Ponder

1. Do you understand acceptance as God describes it? Do you acknowledge that people grow in places they feel accepted?

2. Describe a time when you offered an attitude of acceptance and saw someone soften and respond. Maybe it was you!

3. Do you seek to minister to (serve) your husband? Do you look for his favorites? In what categories besides food can you seek to please him?

4. Write down your husband's two favorite dinners. When was the last time you served these dinners?

5. Take time to discuss how seeking the way to your husband's heart could affect your entire household.

Praying for Each Other

This session can reveal how much hostility can build toward a husband who seeks his own way and does not consider his wife's need or desire for acceptance and for someone to please her with her favorites things. A time of confession may be in order, allowing the Holy Spirit to dig to the bottom of this pain.

Growing Together

1. Choose a topic for the next session. If the work of this lesson does not seem complete, come back to it next week. It is okay to stay with one topic for several sessions.

2. Select or confirm your meeting place and time.

3. Decide together if you want to commit to any specific response between now and your next session. (One gal told me she wanted to cook three meals per week. For her that was a huge step from fast foods and canned soup!)

4. Pray together. This may be an excellent time to kneel together in humility, searching the attitude of your hearts toward serving a husband who takes advantage, or it may be a time to praise God for one who lovingly serves back.

❧ Mentoring Moment ❧

CRAZY WITH LOVE

I know every bump, every bulge, every wrinkle.
Every sag, every bag, every scar,
every flaw, every whisker.
I know that you fleck the bathroom tiles
with shaving foam,
that you flood the floor with bath water,
that you never take your plate out to the sink,

that you strew your clothes,
that you forget to change your socks,
that you tell me the endings of detective novels,
that you track mud through the house,
that you never remember to pay the paper bill.
I know your eccentricities, your prejudices, your
    moods.
And somehow, for some reason
I can never fully understand,
I am crazy with love for you.

— CHARLOTTE GRAY, 1937

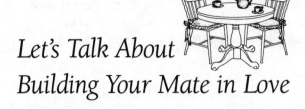

Let's Talk About Building Your Mate in Love

Getting Ready

Plan

Establish your meeting place and the topic of your next session.

Prepare

Read Genesis 2:15-25; 1 Corinthians 11:8,9; 1 John 4:18

Read and meditate on the Scriptures listed above. This session explores ways to build your husband in love. Other sessions on marriage address offering acceptance, being sub-missive, honoring his favorites, and communicating. But in this time together, simply look for ways to build up your husband—God's ways, not yours!

Pray

Father, what are some of the ways You have directed me to build up my husband? Please give me some fresh, new ideas and perspectives on ways to do this. Help me to recognize the times I have torn him down in a selfish attempt to meet my own needs. May I once again be willing to share authentically.

Be Practical

Make a list of some basic building blocks to help your young partner. Don't be too shy to add appropriate intimate tools. Refer to the building of a marriage in terms of construction: Jesus is the foundation, the husband is the center beam.

Our Time Together

Warm Up

Review your topic from the last session. If you have chatted about marriage recently, build on your partner's remarks, prayers, and comments as you begin this session.

Sharing Your Thoughts

Love—pure love, God's love—does cast out fear. Our husbands can be fearful. It is a huge task to take on a wife, children, and home, not to mention a job that requires the biggest bulk of his energy. Demonstrate your pure love so that his fears are assuaged. Offer hope. Listen to his words and his heart.

Watch his body language—look for clues. Speak of the past and future as he gives opportunity, but don't press him to focus on either one. Believe in him. Let him make mistakes without saying, "I told you so." He will be more willing to share the next time. Speak words that lift up and not words that tear down. Offer a place of respite.

In the middle of life's storms, hold on tight, get wet, take huge gulps, and keep holding on until the Storm Calmer Himself, sweet Jesus, calms the waves.

Questions to Ponder

1. Are you certain of God's perfect love? Does it cast out your fears? Describe a specific time when this precious gift was very clear to you.

2. Do you tend to think that only weak people experience fear?

3. Do you acknowledge that fear is a part of your husband's life? Can you recognize the signs?

4. The calming-of-the-seas incident as told in the Gospels shows that God has given Jesus authority to calm the seas. Do you see God using you as a suitable helpmate to calm your husband's seas?

5. List five ways you see your husband as the center beam in your world.

Praying for Each Other

"Lord, I give up all my own plans and purposes, all my own desires and hopes, and accept Thy will for my life. I give myself, my life, my all utterly to Thee to be Thine forever. Fill me and seal me with Thy Holy Spirit. Use me as Thou wilt, send me where Thou wilt, work out Thy whole will in my life at any cost now and forever."

— PRAYER BY BETTY SCOTT STAM

Growing Together

1. Choose a topic, meeting place, and time for your next meeting, and make assignments.

2. Decide if you want to hold each other accountable to perform a specific deed for the purpose of each building her husband in love.

3. Pray together. It is easy to see the need for changes pointed out in this session, but, as always, taking the steps can be more difficult. Remember to ask if there are other prayer concerns in your partner's life.

❦ Mentoring Moment ❦

10 WAYS TO BUILD YOUR HUSBAND IN LOVE

1. *Prepare his breakfast.*

2. *Send him off with a hug and a wave in the morning.*

3. *Stop him and pray for him as he heads for an important meeting.*

4. *Send a treasure in his suitcase, attaché case, or lunch box.*

5. *Write a simple letter and mail it to him.*

6. *Tell him you are going to oil his feet, scratch his back, give him a massage, or whatever calms him, and then do it as planned.*

7. *Listen to him without interrupting.*

8. *Call him at his place of work just to say, "I care about you" or, "I am praying for you."*

9. *Wrap up his favorite snack and put it in his truck or car as he heads to a sporting event.*

10. *Carry his favorite gum, hard candy, or candy bar in your purse when you are going to be together.*

Let's Talk About
Communicating with Your Mate

Getting Ready
Plan
Marriage topics generate lots of interest. Assign the verses below and ask your friend if she would make a list of the trouble spots that she thinks can threaten communication in a marriage.

Prepare
Read Proverbs 14:1; Ephesians 5:33; Philippians 2:3,4,14; Mark 10:7-9; 1 Corinthians 11:11

Read and meditate on the Scriptures listed above. Many fine books have been written on the subject of marriage, and I would suggest you refer to any you have on your bookshelves. If you're looking for new material, try any of these (listed in Supplemental Reading List at the end of this book): *Fit to Be Tied; His Needs, Her Needs; The Language of Love;* and *The Marriage Builder.* A must-read are the chapters about marriage from my book *The Stay-At-Home Mom.*

This is a huge topic, so don't be disappointed if you don't "finish." Communication is never finished!

Pray
Lord of all relationships, the hurts in marriage can be many and can leave deep wounds. I confess my own difficulties in this area and ask for the courage and wisdom to speak truth as I share my victories and failures in communicating with my husband.

Be Practical

Ask your church leaders if they have any quizzes that evaluate communication skills. If not, maybe your local library or bookstore will offer some material. Such tools can help uncover the keys to being a good communicator.

Our Time Together

Warm Up

Review last session's topic and look ahead to other sessions that deal with marriage. Be sensitive to pick up on clues to the strengths and weaknesses in the marriage of your daughter-of-the-heart.

Sharing Your Thoughts

Believe it or not, conflicts about money, children, and even intimacy do not rank higher than poor communication for causing failure in marriage. Learning to express feelings, thoughts, and opinions is difficult. Knowing when to talk and where to share is also very important.

Acknowledge that there are differences in each relationship, but accept the tools that work for all. Here are a few:

> Accept your husband.
>
> Respect your husband.
>
> Regard him as more important than yourself.
>
> Practice timing (when to say what).
>
> Offer humor. Laugh at yourself and help your mate to laugh at himself.
>
> Persevere. Remember, "the common begin, the uncommon finish."

The June 1985 issue of *Psychology Today* includes the article "Marriages Made to Last" by J. Lauer and R. Lauer. They listed these top reasons given by men and women when asked, "What keeps a marriage going?"

Men

My spouse is my best friend.
I like my spouse as a person.
Marriage is a long-term commitment.
Marriage is sacred.
We agree on aims and goals.
My spouse has grown more interesting.
I want the relationship to succeed.
An enduring marriage is important to social stability.
We laugh together.
I am proud of my spouse's achievements.
We agree on a philosophy of life.
We agree about our sex life.
We agree on how and how often to show affection.
I confide in my spouse.
We share outside hobbies and interests.

Women

My spouse is my best friend.
I like my spouse as a person.
Marriage is a long-term commitment.
Marriage is sacred.
We agree on aims and goals.
My spouse has grown more interesting.
I want the relationship to succeed.
We laugh together.
We agree on a philosophy of life.
We agree on how and how often to show affection.
An enduring marriage is important to social stability.
We have a stimulating exchange of ideas.
We discuss things calmly.
We agree about our sex life.
I am proud of my spouse's achievements.

Questions to Ponder

1. Do you sense that your husband keeps ideas, struggles, and joys from you?

2. Is conversation started but sometimes not finished? Do you know why?

3. Are you afraid to bring up sensitive issues with your mate?

4. Can you tell the difference between communication that handles the business of your marriage and communication that promotes growth in your relationship?

5. Did your parents offer a good model in communication?

Praying for Each Other

This is a sensitive issue. Look for ways to affirm. Help your daughter-of-the-heart to see the things that are going well in her marriage. Concentrate on thanking God for His unfailing help.

Growing Together

1. Choose your next session. Try to keep the marriage topics together, but if you can choose a session to enhance the marriage topics, don't hesitate.

2. As always, confirm the time and location for your next meeting.

3. Narrow the broad topic of communication to one or two specifics that need attention in the week to come.

4. Pray together. Ending each session with prayer allows the Holy Spirit to speak to both of you. Allow time to be quiet and listen, as well as time to praise God for all He has given.

Mentoring Moment

I trust you so much that I am able to tell you everything
that I feel and everything that I think
and be certain that it is accepted and understood.
I hope that I may do the same for you
because it is so vital
to be able to share oneself
with someone you trust so much.
My trust for you is so complete.
You can advise me.
You can yell at me.
You can be honest with me.
But please always tell me
whatever you are thinking.
I respect your opinion
as I respect the way you think
and the way you are.

— Author Unknown

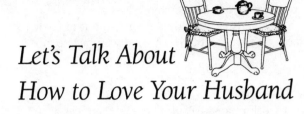

Let's Talk About How to Love Your Husband

Getting Ready

Plan

Find every version you can of the famous passage on love from 1 Corinthians 13. Read each one, noting phrases and words that quicken your heart.

Prepare

Read 1 Corinthians 13

In this session we will dig into God's definition of love as opposed to our own or what we read in the magazines. While other sessions will look at tangibles, this lesson is designed to awaken your heart afresh with the delights of this chapter on love.

Pray

Dearest loving Lord, do I love? Do I seek to clear my heart from frantic self-seeking long enough to express love for You and for the man You sent me to love? May I truly examine my shortcomings in the light of my many blessings.

Be Practical

This is an excellent session to discuss how the concept of love is so often misunderstood. Go to what is familiar for examples. Use your dictionary or women's periodicals to demonstrate how differently God sees and teaches love from the way the heart of man perceives it.

Our Time Together

Warm Up

Review the topic from your last session. This review is extremely important to ensure growth, so don't skip it in favor of the new material. We really only learn what we practice, not what we hear.

Sharing Your Thoughts

The writer of 1 Corinthians is Paul. Like me, Paul was a black-and-white kind of person. He was either in or he was out. First, Paul was dedicated to killing Christians; then, following his acceptance of Jesus, he loved Christians and devoted his life to spreading the Christian faith. Paul's background equipped him to understand and communicate love in a very effective way.

If you were to reduce the Ten Commandments to one word, that word would be *love*. If you love, you will not commit murder or adultery, or take God's name in vain. You will honor your parents and remember to keep the Sabbath holy.

The key characteristics of love described by Paul are patience, kindness, gentleness, humility, courtesy, selflessness, good disposition, guilelessness, and sincerity. Look for these concepts together in 1 Corinthians 13.

Questions to Ponder

1. Did you feel loved as a child? What made you feel loved?

2. Have you at some point accepted notions about love you now see as out of alignment with God's plan? If so, what are they?

3. Which of these key characteristics listed above are the most difficult for you to express? Why?

4. Do you have a choice in love? What is that choice?

5. Take a few minutes to describe a time when you gave and received love with the depth and sincerity we find in this chapter.

Praying for Each Other

Use the answers from questions 2 and 5 to set the tone for your prayer.

Growing Together

1. Choose a topic for the next session and see if there are any assignments, then confirm your meeting place and time.

2. Decide if you want to commit to loving your husband in a particular way between now and your next time together. Example: In response to the chapter on love, I will seek to be more kind to my husband. You may want to memorize a portion of Scripture that will help you in this area. Remember that true love comes out of the heart, and it is the Word hidden in your heart that can give you a new perspective and true love.

3. Pray together. Take a few moments to listen to the voice of God on this very important topic. Touch one another not only in heart but in hand also. Submit your will to Him.

Mentoring Moment

The day you said, 'I do,' you chose your love; since then you have been learning to love your choice."

— AUTHOR UNKNOWN

Let's Talk About How to Simply Submit

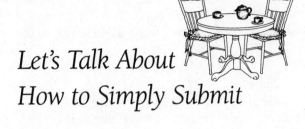

Getting Ready

Plan

When you call to confirm the time and location of your next meeting, point your young friend to any of the passages listed below for reading prior to your appointment. Don't be afraid to change your meeting place if you come up with a better location. Spontaneity can keep the freshness in your times together.

Prepare

Read Hebrews 13:17; Ephesians 5:21-33; Titus 2:3-5;
1 Corinthians 11:3,9

Read and meditate on the selected Scriptures. Consider consulting books or articles on the subject of submission. Key concepts include: obedience, service, yielding, being under authority, subordination, subjection. Some of these terms have military connotations, which add some force to our ideas of submission.

Pray

Father, how am I at submitting? Do I have a servant's heart? For the sake of unity and peace, am I willing to lay down my own ideas and desires? Help me to be forthright and open with my daughter-of-the-heart as we discuss this loaded topic.

Be Practical

The way the concept of submission is viewed by our culture has changed over the years. Look for a newspaper or magazine article that gives an example of lack of submission to authority.

Our Time Together

Warm Up

Review last session's topic. Give an opportunity for responses or questions. Ask at least one question that will lead easily to the topic for today.

Sharing Your Thoughts

Most women have struggled over "giving in" to their husbands and will not find it difficult to contribute to this discussion. Make it clear that dependence on God is essential to successfully "be under" someone else, especially when that person is wrong.

Questions to Ponder

1. What outside sources can help or hinder you from submitting?

2. Describe a time when you saw how being under someone's authority brought peace, unity, or protection.

3. Is your husband the only person you must submit to? If you are not married, should you ever submit to another person?

4. What does God's Word say on this topic? Find at least one applicable Scripture passage.

5. What is a woman's role in the marriage relationship?

Praying for Each Other

Identify at least one area where submission to your husband is particularly difficult and one area where submission to another authority is a struggle, such as obeying the speed limit. Give these areas to God and ask Him to develop in you the submissive spirit that will please Him.

Growing Together

1. Choose your next topic, meeting place, and time, then look for any assignments.

2. Decide if you want to commit to a specific act between now and your next session. Examples: I will pray for the person I have difficulty submitting to; I will submit in one new way to my husband; I will memorize Ephesians 5:21.

3. Pray together. Sit close or kneel together and hold hands as you close your session with a few moments of prayer on the subject of submission.

✹ Mentoring Moment ✹

"Agreement is plan A, submission is plan B."

— BILL EPLEY

Let's Talk About Intimacy

Getting Ready
Plan
Because of the tenderness of this topic, be sure to select your time and place wisely, making sure the choice of location will provide privacy.

Prepare
Read Song of Solomon; 1 Corinthians 7:3-5; 1 Peter 3:7
Read and meditate on the Scriptures listed above. Ed Wheat's book on marriage (*Intended for Pleasure*, Revell Books) is an excellent additional resource. Key thoughts: God's plan for intimacy in marriage; emotional intimacy; physical intimacy; spiritual intimacy; practical ways to nurture intimacy with your mate.

Pray
Father, may the sensitive nature of this topic not hinder our oneness and desire to learn what Your instructions are for married people.

Be Practical
Be open to discussing how American culture views sex, marriage, adultery, and fornication. If these topics are hard for you to talk about, tell your daughter-in-the-Lord and let her lead the discussion. A medical book may be of some help to this conversation.

Our Time Together

Warm Up

I cannot emphasize too much the importance of reviewing the prior topic. You need to provide the opportunity to revisit any topic that your young friend may still be struggling with. This openness to past topics helps your relationship continue to grow.

Then introduce today's topic with some light chatter about boy/girl relationships as teenagers, comparing your era to hers.

Sharing Your Thoughts

Intimacy between two people should be just that: intimate. However, for the sake of this session, encourage your younger friend to share on an appropriate level an evaluation of the intimacy in her marriage. Is her husband satisfied with the frequency of their intimacy? Is she understanding God's clear statement that we no longer have charge over our own bodies, but rather our mate has charge over us?

Marriage has many levels of acceptance. When we open our hearts to our husbands, then we allow them access to our emotions. Wedding vows are traditionally sealed with a kiss; that kiss signifies the admittance to the physical level between man and woman. Help your young friend to see how the plan of marriage compares to Jesus' relationship to the Church.

Questions to Ponder

1. Would spending more time with your mate help the intimate side of your relationship?

2. What are some actions that could promote intimacy with your mate?

3. Do you have any fears regarding this area of your marriage?

4. Do you have any history that would affect your marriage relationship? If yes, do not feel you must discuss this together in your session, but be certain to express this to God and anyone involved so that healing can take place.

5. Do you have good verbal communication with your mate?

Praying for Each Other

Be careful not to betray any confidences shared during your prayer request time.

Growing Together

1. It's time to choose another meeting time and place, as well as another topic. The rest of the topics will look a bit easier now that this one is behind you. Be confident of the work God has done in your time with this young woman.

2. Pray with compassion. The serious impact of what goes on behind closed doors is dramatic. Both you and your daughter-of-the-heart need to be mindful of the potential pain involved in marriage and intimacy.

❧ Mentoring Moment ❧

How do I love thee? Let me count the ways.
I love thee to the depth and breadth and height
My soul can reach, when feeling out of sight
For the ends of Being and ideal Grace.
I love thee to the level of everyday's
Most quiet need, by sun and candle-light.
I love thee freely, as men strive for Right;
I love thee purely, as they turn from Praise.
I love thee with the passion put to use
In my griefs, and with my childhood's faith.
I love thee with a love I seemed to lose
With my lost saints. I love thee with the breath,
Smiles, tears, of all my life! And, if God choose,
I shall but love thee better after death.
　　　　　　　　　　— ELIZABETH BARRETT BROWNING

Let's Talk About Diagnosing Your Children

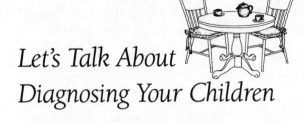

Getting Ready

Plan
Send your young friend a cute card or note to remind her of your next meeting. Let her know that your sessions together minister to you as well. Encourage her regarding your last topic of discussion.

Prepare
Read 1 Corinthians 10:31; 7:7; Proverbs 22:29; Romans 12:3-8; 1 Corinthians 12; Proverbs 22:6; Two Sides of Love; The Treasure Tree; *and* Please Understand Me *(see Supplemental Reading List at the back of the book).*

Read and meditate on the Scriptures listed above, and refer to the suggested materials as possible.

Pray
Lord, let me honestly examine how I am using what You have given me. I thank You for the privilege of bringing glory to my King with the good gifts You have granted.

Be Practical
Consider the additional material for this section. If you have access to these resources, this may be the time to complete a personality profile, temperament evaluation, or spiritual gifts inventory. Many churches have these tools available.

Our Time Together

Warm Up

Review last session's topic. Be ready to dig deeper into issues that are important to the young woman God has directed to you.

Sharing Your Thoughts

Have you ever suffered from an ailment? Of course! We have all experienced common colds and flu viruses, at the very least. When these illnesses attack, we know what to do: take aspirins, drink plenty of fluids, and rest.

But what if you suffer from recurring headaches? Those painful symptoms are persistent, and you may fail to find any relief until one day a doctor pronounces, "These headaches are caused by poor vision." You order the new glasses he prescribes, and, *voila*, Headaches are gone. But not until the proper diagnosis is achieved do you find a course of direction that leads to eventual relief.

Raising children is just like that. It is essential to find out who they are, how they are "bent" in terms of temperament, environment, spiritual gifts (for those who have chosen Jesus), interests, and natural talents. All of these factors will help you direct this precious gift from God. (I suggest you pick up a copy of Doug and Katie Fortune's book *Discovering Your Children's Motivational Gifts.*)

For example, if your child is naturally talkative, God may use him or her to preach or teach. You will want to encourage this child's language skills and temper excessive verbal communication so that this gift will be a blessing to others.

Get the picture? Help your daughter-of-the-heart commit to this task for her children . . . perhaps even for herself and her mate!

Questions to Ponder

1. Did you ever ask yourself why your children are so different from one another? From yourself? Now that you know the reason, how will this knowledge assist you in nurturing the character and potential of each little personality?

2. Was this information a part of your growing up? If not, can you see how it might have helped you? Describe.

3. What do you believe your spiritual gifts are? Are you using them faithfully?

4. Give a short profile of each of your family members.

5. If you have recognized something new about anyone in your family, describe how this new diagnosis will help you deal with that family member.

Praying for Each Other

It does take time and energy to observe and listen to children in order to discover why they do some of the things they do. Ask God to give you energy and time to dig deeper. You may need to rearrange your schedule for a time to make these important evaluations.

Growing Together

1. Select your next session time, topic, location, and check for any advance assignments.

2. Perhaps today's session challenged you to take action. If so, take the time now to create a plan for that action.

3. Pray together.

❧ Mentoring Moment ☙

A PRAYER FOR YOUR CHILDREN

"Lord, I thank You for the gifts and talents you have placed in (name of child) _____.
I pray that You would develop them in _____
(name of child) and use them for Your glory. Make them apparent to me and to him or her, and show me specifically if there is any special nurturing, training, learning experience, or opportunities I should provide for him or her.

May his or her gifts and talents be developed in Your way and in Your time.

"Your Word says, 'Having then gifts differing according to the grace that is given to us, let us use them' (Romans 12:6). As he or she recognizes the talents and abilities You've given him or her, I pray that no feelings of inadequacy, fear, or uncertainty will keep him or her from using them according to Your will. May he or she hear the call You have on his or her life so that he or she doesn't spend a lifetime trying to figure out what it is or miss it altogether. Let the talents never be wasted, watered down by mediocrity, or used to glorify anything or anyone other than You, Lord.

"I pray that You would reveal to my child what his or her life work is to be and help him or her excel in it. Bless the work of his or her hands and may he or she be able to earn a good living doing the work he or she loves and does best.

"Your Word says that 'A man's gift makes room for him, and brings him before great men' (Proverbs 18:16). May whatever my child does find favor with others and be well received and respected. But most of all, I pray the gifts and talents You placed in this child be released to find their fullest expression in glorifying You."

— STORMIE OMARTIAN
The Power of a Praying Parent

Let's Talk About Training the Will of Your Children

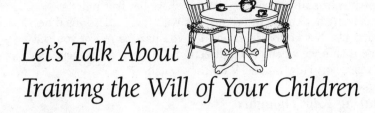

Getting Ready

Plan

When you call or write to confirm the time and location of your next meeting, encourage your friend to read the Deuteronomy passage below before you get together.

Prepare

Read Deuteronomy 6:6-10; Proverbs 22:6; Genesis 14:14; Colossians 3:21. For further study, refer to What Is a Family? *by Edith Schaeffer.*

Read and meditate on the assigned materials. Think about how your mother trained you and how you trained your children. Research and meditate on the differences between training and teaching.

Pray

Lord, reveal to me any mistakes in child training that I have made but have not acknowledged or confessed. Show me if and to whom I need to make restitution, and give me the strength and courage to do so. Help me to direct this young woman to You, the most true Parent, for her instruction and training.

Be Practical

Photocopy chapters 6 and 7 out of *The Stay-At-Home Mom,* or clip relevant articles on child training from Christian magazines to give your younger partner.

Our Time Together

Warm Up

Ask your daughter-of-the-heart to share her frustrations concerning her children. Prompt her with these questions if necessary: Do they go to bed easily? Do you have to repeat yourself more than once when giving directions? Do they keep their rooms clean? How much TV do they watch?

Sharing Your Thoughts

The Hebrew word for "train" literally means to "rub the gullet." The word refers to a primitive practice of opening an infant's throat by pouring a liquid such as blood or saliva into the throat and then rubbing the outside of the throat. This prompted the child to breathe and swallow.

Training is different from teaching. Because young children do not have the cognitive ability to reason, training is a necessary and important step in their growth. For a two-year-old to respond to your "no," you must first have trained him or her to do so without teaching the reason for saying no. That teaching will come later. A child who is trained early is always more able to be trained by the voice of God when he or she becomes accountable.

Questions to Ponder

1. Do you believe there are limitations in training a child? Why?

2. What are your ideas about breaking a child's spirit versus training his or her will?

3. How did your parents train you?

4. Describe a way you show your children you respect them.

5. Read each of the following situations and determine if the parental response in each situation represents one or more of these: (a) breaking the spirit; (b) encouraging the spirit; (c) negatively reinforcing the will; or (d) shaping the will. Try to come to some consensus in each situation. Think of ways the parental response could be improved.

   • Four-year-old Jessie spills her milk at supper while reaching for the butter, after she has been told twice to ask for what she wants. You immediately say, "Now what did you have to do that for?" You get up and clean up the mess yourself.

- Five-year-old David yells, "No, I won't!" when you tell him to come back and take his water toys out of the bathtub. You respond, "Until you pick up those toys, I won't let you play with Johnny."

- Your fifteen-year-old has forgotten to fold the laundry while watching a special TV program for three hours last night. You ask him to do it when he gets home from school tonight instead of doing it yourself.

- Your nine-year-old repeatedly fails to make her bed before leaving for school in the morning, despite your instruction and training. You are expecting guests, so you make the bed for her.

- Your three-year-old refuses to eat the dinner placed before him. After trying to entice him to eat his favorite foods, you send him to his room without dinner.

Praying for Each Other
Pray for any training God may need to do in your own lives. It is never too late to be changed in the presence of a holy God. Pray for all the children God has placed in your lives, including daughters- and sons-of-the-heart.

Growing Together
1. Help your young partner identify a specific area in which she needs to train or retrain her child. Determine one thing she can do to begin the process.

2. Look at the topic you will discuss in your next meeting. Make any assignments that will make your meeting more productive.

3. Agree on your next meeting place and time.

4. Pray together. Hold hands and ask your heavenly Father to make your eyes and minds clear to all the training He wants to accomplish in your lives. Ask God to bless your young

friend as she seeks to train her children effectively and lovingly in the ways of God.

❧ Mentoring Moment ❧

If a child lives with criticism
He learns to condemn.
If a child lives with hostility
He learns to fight.
If a child lives with ridicule
He learns to be shy.
If a child lives with shame
He learns to feel guilty.
If a child lives with tolerance
He learns to be patient.
If a child lives with encouragement
He learns confidence.
If a child lives with praise
He learns justice.
If a child lives with security
He learns to have faith.
If a child lives with approval
He learns to like himself.
If a child lives with acceptance and
*   friendship*
He learns to find love in the world.
— DOROTHY LAW NOLTE

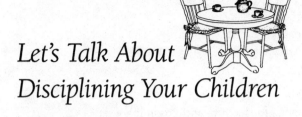

Let's Talk About Disciplining Your Children

Getting Ready

Plan
When you schedule the time and location of your next meeting, ask your young friend to be thinking about her children and how they respond to discipline.

Prepare
Read Ephesians 6:1-4

Read and meditate on the Scripture listed above. The topic of discipline can be complicated and controversial, so be careful to stick to God's Word and your own experiences. Prepare your heart to share how disciplined you are personally. Also be ready to talk about how you disciplined your children.

Pray
Father in heaven, do I obey You and please You? Make my heart more in tune to obedience and discipline than ever before.

Be Practical
While it is generally not a good idea to compare one child with another, it is helpful to have a means of measuring the growth of each child you are responsible to raise. Prior to this session, you might prepare a chart that will show areas of maturity children should achieve at certain ages and phases of life. For example:

Age 2-3:
- Pick up toys
- Put things back where they belong
- Brush teeth
- Pull covers off the bed
- Pick up toys

Age 4:
- set the table
- Be responsible for feeding and grooming a pet
- Make simple sandwich or cold cereal breakfast
- Help with housework: push vacuum, dust furniture

Age 5:
- Help with dinner preparation: tear lettuce, butter bread
- Make bed
- Scour sink
- Make phone calls

Age 6:
- Choose clothing
- Keep room in order
- Prepare school lunch
- Tie own shoes
- Help mom or dad with more complicated cleaning jobs

Age 7:
- Take phone messages
- Water lawn
- Carry in the groceries
- Do flat ironing (use hankies and napkins—so the children can iron them!)

Age 8:
- Be responsible for personal hygiene
- Sew on a button or mend a tear
- Help with cooking: read recipes, learn cooking instructions
- Help with young children
- Polish silver
- Sweep walkways

Age 9-10:
- Do chores without reminders
- Have a pen pal
- Help with the grocery shopping
- Clean bedroom and bath (vacuum, dust, scrub tub and toilets)
- Learn more about money management

Age 11:
- Earn money: babysitting, mother's helper, yard work
- Learn about banking
- Have a clothing allowance

Our Time Together
Warm Up
Review! Review! Review! Don't skip this essential part of the process. It gives you an opportunity to hear the heart of this young woman, and it gives her the chance to follow up on issues that especially interest or challenge her. Review also helps you to be accountable to each other for what you are learning together.

Sharing Your Thoughts
When you honor someone, you show merited respect. We are told by God to honor our parents simply because God put them in that position. Some parents have not earned that honor by deed and word. But here we see clearly that it is not the action that grants them honor, but rather the title of parent that God has bestowed.

It will be valuable to discuss how your young friend dealt with her own parents. This is a session that can assist both of you in the area of personal discipline.

Elisabeth Elliot said, "Anything less than instant obedience is disobedience." Two key issues to discuss are: How fast do your children respond to your directives and do they obey fully? Partial obedience is not accepted by God (see 1 Samuel 15— Saul and Agag) and should not be accepted by a parent. This training should start early, but it is never too late to start expecting obedience from our children. It is never too late to begin learning and increasing our own levels of obedience.

Questions to Ponder

1. Do you view the word "discipline" as the "D" word? Try to discover why.

2. Have you ever read any books or attended any seminars on the subject of disciplining your children? Describe.

3. Do you understand the term "reality discipline"? Do you practice reality discipline?

4. Are you and your husband in agreement about how to raise and discipline your children? If not, what do you think is God's response to your lack of agreement?

5. Discuss the impact of inadequate discipline in the family on your community and the world at large.

Praying for Each Other

It is easier for children to learn order and discipline from a mother who is orderly and disciplined. Pray that your daughter-in-the-Lord will want to lead the way by her willingness to honor God and her own parents. Pray for the courage to live a disciplined life of obedience to God.

Growing Together

1. Agree on a meeting place, time, and topic for your next visit. Look for any advance assignments.

2. Decide if you want to commit to a specific response to the topic of the week. For example, you may choose to memorize Ephesians 6:1-4.

3. Pray together. Let your hearts draw close as you hold your friend's hands, kneel side by side, or put your arm around her shoulder during your last few minutes of prayer.

Mentoring Moment

"If we had paid no more attention to our plants than we have to our children, we would now be living in a jungle of weeds."

— LUTHER BURBANK, PRIOR TO 1923

Let's Talk About
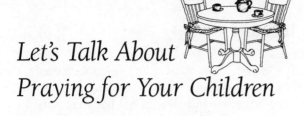
Praying for Your Children

Getting Ready
Plan
Arrange your upcoming time with your daughter-of-the-heart. Suggest that she become familiar with the verses and material below in order to prepare her heart for this topic.

Prepare
Read Exodus 20:12; Deuteronomy 6:5-9; Psalm 78:5-7;
1 Samuel 1 and 2; and The-Stay-At-Home Mom, pp. 60-63.

Read and meditate on the assigned Scriptures and refer to the suggested material. If you have any material on the topic of prayer or specific prayers for children, incorporate that information into this session. This will be an excellent time to acknowledge others who have prayed for you or your children and to remember the prayers you prayed as you raised your children.

Pray
Once again, Lord, I humble myself before You. Help me to recall how I prayed on behalf of my children, how often I did so, and how You answered those prayers. Please use me to instill a determination in the heart of this young woman to be found faithful in praying for her children.

Be Practical
This session would be an appropriate time to help your young friend set up a prayer notebook. Keep it simple: Notebook paper and three-ring binders are always available, inexpensive, and easy

to use. Perhaps you could shop together for these items, or you might want to give them as a gift.

Our Time Together

Warm Up

Review your topic from last session. If follow-up is desired, take time to revisit the information. Ask your young friend a question or two about the role of prayer in her life, then transition into the topic of praying for her children.

Sharing Your Thoughts

The Bible tells us that we are all born sinners. As mothers, it is important for us to recognize the sinful condition of our children's hearts even at birth. As we acknowledge their lost condition, we can begin to pray immediately for their future conversion. In addition to praying, we can teach and train by example and by word the life-giving truths of Christ's life, death on the cross for our sins, resurrection, and ascension into heaven.

Biblical illustrations of the power of prayer to change hearts are plentiful. God has granted us the responsibility to train, protect, and pray for our children. When, how, or where we pray is not as important as our commitment to pray individually and regularly for each of our gifts from God.

Questions to Ponder

1. Is prayer a regular part of your life? If so, describe how you established the priority of prayer in your life. If not, describe your efforts and difficulties in this area.

2. Who was, or is, the single most influential person in your spiritual journey? Has that person prayed for you?

3. Reflect on an answer to prayer that occurred in the last six months.

4. Have you ever written your prayers? If not, are you willing to give it a try?

5. Do you pray with your children as well as for your children?

Praying for Each Other

Today I would suggest that you take the time to pray for at least half of the eighteen recommended prayer topics taken from *The Stay-At-Home Mom* and found on p. 137 of this book. This discipline will serve your children well. Such a prayer time also enriches the relationship of those praying together.

Growing Together

1. Choose your topic for the next session and examine it for any assignments.

2. Select or confirm your next meeting place and time.

3. For the coming week, ask your young partner to complete the eighteen prayers for her children that you began together today. She should come prepared to chat about the experience during the next session's review time.

4. Pray together. What a privilege it is to hear the heart of another human being! As you pray for your children, you will find a new and deeper bond.

❧ Mentoring Moment ❧

PRAYER FOR OUR CHILDREN

"Father, hear us, we are praying,
Hear the words our hearts are saying,
We are praying for our children.

Keep them from the power of evil,
From the secret hidden peril,
Father, hear us for our children.

From the whirlpool that would suck them,
From the treacherous quicksand, pluck them,
Father, hear us for our children.
From the worldling's hollow gladness

From the sting of faithless sadness,
Father, Father, keep our children.

Through life's troubled waters, steer them,
Through life's bitter battles cheer them,
Father, Father be thou near them.

Read the language of our longing,
Read the wordless pleadings thronging
Holy Father for our children.

And wherever they may bide,
   lead them home at eventide."

— AMY CARMICHAEL

Let's Talk About the Ministry of Motherhood

Getting Ready

Plan

It is necessary to confirm each week the time and location of your meeting and to encourage your young friend to read the suggested passages of Scripture.

Prepare

Read Psalm 127:1,3,5; Proverbs 31; 14:1

Read and meditate on the Scriptures listed above. Chapter 3 of *The Stay-At-Home Mom* is the basis of this lesson time.

Pray

From the works of Edith Schaeffer to Erma Bombeck, millions of words have been written about motherhood. Jesus, take my heart and mind and reshape them to look like Your mother's. Mary said to the angel, "Let it be to me according to your word," and the world was changed. May I be the kind of mother who wants God's will first.

Be Practical

This session will go so fast that you may want to plan ahead and spend two meetings on this topic. Perhaps making a list of related topics of interest would help sharpen the focus. Your list might include: breast feeding, demand versus scheduled feeding, spanking, children's books and toys, and education. (Training the will of your children is covered in another session.)

Our Time Together

Warm Up

Once again—review! If you have already discussed more than five of these sessions, you may want to go back and review some earlier topics to discover how helpful your time together has been and to share the blessings.

Sharing Your Thoughts

Children are a gift from God. He uses them to mold your character, just as He will use you to shape them. Sarah Edwards and her husband, Jonathan, had 1400 descendants. The list of their accomplishments is notable. These descendants include a United States Vice President, 13 college presidents, 65 professors, and 66 doctors.

While these accomplishments are extraordinary, the single most important task you can do for your children is to lead them to Jesus Christ. Education, credentials, and experiences do not mean as much as one simple confession of sin and acknowledgment of need for a Savior.

To minister is to serve. As mothers, our primary task is to serve our families—not as slaves, but as willing servants.

Enjoy together this poem written by Kathi Mills in her book *Mommy, Where Are You?*

MEMORIES OF MOTHER

When all the children have grown and gone,
Which memories of Mother will linger on?
Will it be the times she dried their tears,
Held them close, and calmed their fears?

The way she always found the time
To read their favorite nursery rhyme
Over and over, time and again,
Until they knew it, beginning to end.

The sleepless nights with an ailing child,
Mother stayed there all the while,
Ministering love with healing hands,
Spinning tales of faraway lands.

What memories will follow them as they go?
All of these, and more, I know;
But most important can they say,
"She loved God's Word and taught me to pray"?

Questions to Ponder

1. Is the idea of motherhood as a ministry a new idea to you? In a few sentences, describe motherhood.

2. To what authorities do you answer as a wife and mother? Please list them in order.

3. Name the top five challenges you face as a mother.

4. What is the most thrilling part of being a mother in your home?

5. What did your mother do that you would like to repeat? Not repeat?

Praying for Each Other

For most young women the delight of being a mother is never-ending, and yet each day holds difficulties and decisions that mothers feel ill-equipped to handle. Make this time of prayer a time of celebrating motherhood and the fact that God trusts His children to our care. Dwell on what an honor it is to be called "mother." When the session is complete, you and your daughter-of-the-heart want to have God's perspective on this often overwhelming responsibility.

Growing Together

1. Choose your next topic for exploration. Check for any advance assignments.

2. For a change, adopt a new meeting place. Perhaps you could meet in the park or at a coffeehouse.

3. Decide if there is anything you want to ask this young woman to accomplish relating to the subject of being a minister to her children. It is not necessary to assign a task weekly, but from time to time it will help her stay on track.

4. Pray together over this important topic of mothering. Commit to our God the issues that trouble you in your attempt to please Him in your mothering role. Rejoice over His gifts, His hand of protection, and His omniscience in your family life.

Mentoring Moment

There is a well known song by Brent Lamb and John Rosasco which refers to building a household of faith. The lyrics describe the household standing through strong winds because it is built by husband and wife together with God's help. Consider the example to children that is set by godly parents who seek to build a household of faith together, one that withstands the storms of life because it is founded on Christ.

Let's Talk About
Learning to Love Your Children

Getting Ready

Plan

Make sure that your young friend has had a full week to study the assigned verses for this very important session. Call her to confirm the time and location of your meeting.

Prepare

Read 1 John 4:7,8,21; 1 Corinthians 13; Proverbs 17:5; Mark 1:40-42; Philippians 4:8; Isaiah 66:12; Proverbs 21:19; Proverbs 15:15

Read and meditate on the Scriptures listed above. The abundant material covers the concept of love and can be applied to practical ways a mother can love her children.

Pray

Dearest Lord Jesus, You are Love. You demonstrate that love every day and every way in the lives of all You have created. Help me to be a channel of Your love to this young woman in my life. Help us to discover ways to offer love to our children.

Be Practical

Do you have any poems about children, any books that talk about the ways to love and cherish children? If so, spend a little time in this material. When this session is over, both of you should have a deeper sense of how God would like His children to be loved.

Our Time Together

Warm Up

Review last session's topic. Talk briefly about what it was like to grow up in your family, and ask your friend to share a bit about her childhood.

Sharing Your Thoughts

Keep your children in mind as you explore the following expressions of love, all of which can be found in Scripture:

Give the choice of love. Commit to love because it is right, not because it feels good.

Give the words of love. We all need regular verbal assurance, but children need it the most.

Give the touch of love. Research has confirmed the human need for physical touch. The need to be held and cuddled is especially critical for babies.

Give the encouragement of love. "Put courage into" those little people by letting them know that you are their best fan and cheerleader.

Give the comfort of love. In times of pain or sadness, love offers healing comfort.

Give the laughter of love. Laughter sets a pleasant mood, a bright tone. Make merriment a daily dose of love in your home.

Give the discipline of love. Discipline establishes boundaries for children, making them feel safe and secure.

Questions to Ponder

1. Have you ever felt unloving toward your children? All mothers do at times. Describe why this feeling bothered you.

2. With which of the above expressions of love do you struggle the most? Do you know why? If so, discuss it with your friend.

3. Do you expect or desire for your children to love and honor you?

4. Can you think back to something you learned to love as a child? What was it? How did you learn to love it?

5. Together, make a short list of ways you love your children.

Praying for Each Other

Share about a time you felt loved as a child, then share about a time you felt rejected. Ask God to use those experiences to mold you into a loving person today and in the future.

Growing Together

1. Choose the time, location, and topic of your next meeting, and see if there are any advance assignments.

2. Did something in this session inspire you to respond in a specific way? Perhaps you would like to write a love letter to one of your children or maybe you can commit to touch each of them at least once a day. Then do it!

3. Pray together.

✻ Mentoring Moment ✻

Sing together "Jesus Loves the Little Children" and "Jesus Loves Me."

Let's Talk About the Ministry of Your Mansion

Getting Ready

Plan

Be prepared to discuss "mansions" (homes) for this session. If you have been meeting in her mansion, maybe you should have this session at your mansion. Or borrow the mansion of someone you know who has a great bent toward hospitality. Be creative.

Prepare

Read Matthew 12:34,35; Proverbs 17:1; 1 Peter 4:9,10; John 14:2,3

Read and meditate on the Scriptures listed above. Collect some magazines like *House Beautiful* or *Victoria*. If you can secure a copy of *Open Heart, Open Home* by Karen Mains, scan it for inspiration. Is your mansion full of mercy—or misery?

Pray

Lord, I am grateful to You for my dwelling place. Whatever its size or location, I want my mansion to be a place of mercy. Please sensitize me to the effect my home has on those who live and visit there. Let me examine my level of investment as a servant to the people I love.

Be Practical

This is a grand time to talk about comforts in the home and concepts of quiet, peace, and preparation. You might want to review other sessions that deal with the home in terms of traditions, menus, and organization.

Our Time Together

Warm Up

Review last session's topic. Share photos you may have collected out of magazines and talk about how color, design, and texture can create certain feelings and effects.

Sharing Your Thoughts

A woman's mansion is most often a reflection of herself. Do the members of your family feel grace and mercy, love and acceptance in your home? Or do they sense misery, critical thinking, judgment, and aloofness? This ministry is intended first to the people who live in your house, and then to the guests who visit.

Whether your visitor is dropping in for a fifteen-minute cup of coffee, attending a formal dinner party, or staying in your guest room for two weeks, consider how to prepare your heart and home for ministry. The hospitality you deliver is a direct result of your heart condition. Hospitality is not the act of fixing a meal; it is opening a door, offering a smile, and bringing comfort to one of God's creatures. The service you provide to your family will comfort them, and the service offered to your guest will comfort your family and your guest.

Reach out—offer mercy, not misery.

Questions to Ponder

1. Are you available to meet the needs of your family members? Or does your self-imposed schedule conflict with their needs?

2. List five ways you serve your family daily. With what attitude is that service given?

3. When a guest arrives, does it seem like an intrusion? If so, examine why you react this way.

4. What was the mood of the home in which you grew up?

5. Reflect on mansions you love to visit.

Praying for Each Other

This is an excellent time to admit that we cannot always be "Miss Mercy" and that it is unrealistic to expect to serve with a consistent amount of zeal. Ask God to reveal how mercy looks in action. Submit a bitter heart to the Healer for softening and reshaping.

Growing Together

1. Look ahead to your next meeting time, location, and topic, and see if there are any assignments you should consider.

2. Decide if you want to commit to any specific steps in an effort to bring a fresh ministry to your mansion.

3. Pray together.

❧ Mentoring Moment ❧

A Parting Guest

"What delightful hosts they are—
Life and love!
Lingeringly I turn away,
This late hour, yet glad enough
They have not withheld from me
Their high hospitality.
So with face lit with delight
And all gratitude, I stay
Yet to press their hands and say,
"Thanks. So fine a time! Good night."
— James Whitcomb Riley

Oh what joy to have every family member and guest respond in this manner!

Let's Talk About
Being the Keeper of Your Home

Getting Ready
Plan
Give your younger partner a reminder call regarding the date, time, and topic of your next meeting in her mansion. Ask her to read the verses for this session and to evaluate her own home on the basis of clutter, cleanliness, and orderliness.

Prepare
Read Proverbs 31; Titus 2:3-5; Philippians 3:13,14

Read and meditate on the Scriptures listed. You may want to read my book *Get More Done in Less Time* and to give or loan a copy to your young friend. Be ready to discuss priorities, order, and any and all practical housekeeping tips.

Pray
Lord, help me to see the connection between Your orderly creation and our need to desire and cultivate order in our lives. Let me be willing to admit to a messy closet or confused filing system as we try to help each other in this area. No matter how organized I am, help me to see there is always room for more order.

Be Practical
Prepare some visual aids, such as pot holders, laundry sorting bags, purse organization pouches, a daily planner, children's toy sorters, feather dusters, polishes and cleaners, or other time-saving tools.

Our Time Together

Warm Up

Review last session's topic, making sure that your communication of past material has been effective. Ask your younger partner about her mother's style of housekeeping and how she may continue to be affected by it.

Sharing Your Thoughts

Talk about which of these names best characterizes you: Messy Maggie, Confused Carol, or Neat Nancy. Try to describe how your family is affected by these traits. Be sensitive to the fact that we all keep our homes differently, and there is no one "right way." However, God's Word does indicate that we should keep peace, keep records, keep order, and keep persevering. These are prerequisites for a healthy, peaceful home and can be applied even to such mundane tasks as daily maintenance of kitchens, bathrooms, and bedrooms. Furthermore, keeping accurate financial records is essential to being good stewards.

Questions to Ponder

1. Are you prepared to invite people to your home spontaneously? If not, why?

2. Have you ever looked in vain for something you knew you had?

3. Do you spend time going over the same paperwork more than once because what you need is in a pile somewhere?

4. Do you have more than one unfinished project from the past two years?

5. Do you feel burdened with too many things to accomplish?

6. Is it hard for you to say "No"?

Praying for Each Other

Ask God for the courage to submit one messy place in your home to Him. It may be a car full of junk, photos that need to be mounted in albums, a catch-all drawer in the kitchen, or the top shelf of your closet. Seek joy from the Lord in the process of bringing order from chaos.

Growing Together

1. Where do you want to go from here? Select a topic that fits your needs and look for an assignment.

2. Establish your next meeting time and place.

3. Decide if you want to commit to cleaning up the area you prayed about.

4. Pray together. Let the frustrations of undone work spill out of your hearts. Acknowledge that you can put past failures behind you and move ahead to apply principles of order.

✄ Mentoring Moment ✄

"It is not what you do that makes you tired, but what you don't do."

— DONNA OTTO

Let's Talk About Food, Menus, and Hospitality

Getting Ready

Plan

Clear enough time on your schedule to do this session as a project, if possible. Invite your young friend to join you in planning a menu, making a shopping list, and doing the marketing. This will be fun for both of you.

Prepare

Read Proverbs 31; Titus 2:3-5; 1 Peter 4:9; Romans 12:13

Read and meditate on the Scriptures above. Read chapters 5 and 14 of *Get More Done in Less Time*. In case you don't have access to this book, two forms which are a part of chapter 5 are also included at the end of this session so that you can copy those for your young friend.

Pray

Father, You ask us to redeem the time and be good stewards of our money. May this extremely practical session help us to make good use of the time and money available to us.

Be Practical

Ahead of time, prepare a menu plan for one week as an example to share with your daughter-of-the-heart. You can leave this menu plan with her at the conclusion of your time together. Pull out a few of your favorite recipes, making sure that some are easy. It might also be fun to introduce your young friend to your favorite kitchen tools and tell her why you find them so useful.

Our Time Together

Warm Up

This is a very full session, so keep your review to a minimum. You may even want to table the review until your next meeting. Start your conversation by talking about house-guests, having company for dinner, and throwing parties. Share your greatest defeat and your greatest victory in these categories!

Sharing Your Thoughts

Together, prepare a menu plan for your young friend's week, including breakfasts and dinners. As you make the plan, use your market list to circle and check the items you will need to prepare each of these meals. Then, when you get to the market, make certain your head is not turned by a pretty bunch of asparagus—unless asparagus is on your list!

The topic of hospitality is very important to the heart of God. As His people, we are His hands. Hospitality starts with hands that hold doors open for others in public places, pat small children with affection, and touch someone's shoulder or arm when a moment of comfort is needed. These same hands are to maintain an orderly home and prepare a meal to serve daily to our families and occasionally to guests, sometimes even "angels unaware." (See *They Didn't Know They Were Angels* by Doris Greig, Regal Books.)

This art of hospitality must not be lost. Encourage this younger woman to open her doors often to anyone God may send. We should not wait for the "right time" or the "right stuff." If we do, we may lose a blessing.

Questions to Ponder

1. Did you grow up in a home that welcomed people, or one that made them feel uncomfortable?

2. Do you feel it is just too much work to prepare for extra guests in your home?

3. What do you think the Scripture means when it tells us to

practice hospitality without grumbling and complaining? Why do you think we do grumble and complain?

4. What is your biggest fear about having guests for dinner? What can you actively do about this concern?

5. If you have planned menus in the past, why did you stop?

6. Discuss a party that you went to (small or large, in a home or public place) that made you smile. What ingredients did the event offer?

Praying for Each Other

For us older women it is easy to put aside regular meal preparation and the habit of opening our homes to others. After all, we did our part already, right? For young women it is easy to believe that there will be many other opportunities and that they should wait until the dishes match. Ask God to give both of you the energy and desire to share all that belongs to Him with others.

Growing Together

1. Choose your next meeting time, place, and topic. Check advance assignments.

2. Decide to complete one more menu planner before you meet again. Remember to use pencil on your planner so you can erase and use the same plan again.

3. Pray together. This practical information has a way of changing our focus. As we become more efficient we have more energy and time for effectiveness.

❧ Mentoring Moment ❧

BROCCOLI CHOWDER
by Donna Otto
(I serve this chowder every Thanksgiving.)

Ingredients

2 pounds fresh broccoli
3 12½ oz. cans chicken broth
2 cups milk
l cup chopped, cooked (shaved) ham

2 tsp. salt
¼ tsp. pepper (white preferred)
l cup light cream
½ pound Swiss cheese, grated
¼ cup butter

Instructions

In a large covered kettle cook broccoli in one can of chicken broth for about seven minutes, or until tender. Remove broccoli from broth, cool and chop coarsely. Add remaining chicken broth, milk, ham, salt, and pepper. Bring to boil over medium heat, stirring occasionally. Stir in remaining ingredients, adding light cream last. Be sure not to boil after cream is added as it will curdle.

Menu Planner   Date:

	Breakfast	Lunch	Dinner
S U N			
M O N			
T U E S			
W E D			
T H U R			
F R I			
S A T			

Shopping Checklist

	Qty	Cost	Cp*
FROZEN FOOD/JUICE			
Ice Cream	___	___	___
	___	___	___
Vegetables	___	___	___
	___	___	___
	___	___	___
	___	___	___
	___	___	___
	___	___	___
Prepared			
Dinners	___	___	___
	___	___	___
Juice	___	___	___
	___	___	___
	___	___	___
CONDIMENTS			
Syrup	___	___	___
Molasses	___	___	___
Jelly/Jams	___	___	___
Peanut Butter	___	___	___
Honey	___	___	___
Shortening	___	___	___
Oil	___	___	___
Catsup	___	___	___
Mustard	___	___	___
Vinegar	___	___	___
Mayonnaise	___	___	___
Pickles	___	___	___
Relish	___	___	___
Salad Dressing	___	___	
Croutons	___	___	___
CANNED GOODS			
Soups	___	___	___
	___	___	___
Canned Meat	___	___	___
Tuna	___	___	___
Canned Meals	___	___	___
CANNED VEGETABLES			
Tomato Sauce/			
Paste	___	___	___
Vegetables	___	___	___
	___	___	___
	___	___	___
	___	___	___
	___	___	___
	___	___	___
	___	___	___
	___	___	___

	Qty	Cost	Cp
STAPLES			
Flour	___	___	___
Sugar	___	___	
Cereal	___	___	
	___	___	___
Mixes	___	___	
Nuts	___	___	
Jello	___	___	
SPICES			
Bacon Bits	___	___	___
Coconut	___	___	___
Chocolate	___	___	___
Baking Soda	___	___	___
Baking Powder	___	___	___
Salt/Pepper	___	___	___
	___	___	___
	___	___	___
	___	___	___
	___	___	___
PASTA			
Spaghetti	___	___	___
Pasta	___	___	___
Rice	___	___	___
Instant			
Potatoes	___	___	___
Mixes	___	___	___
	___	___	___
	___	___	___
DRINKS			
Coffee	___	___	___
Tea	___	___	___
Juice	___	___	___
	___	___	___
Sparkling			
Colas	___	___	___
	___	___	___
	___	___	___
	___	___	___
	___	___	___
PASTRY			
Crackers	___	___	___
Cookies	___	___	___
Chips	___	___	___
Breads	___	___	___
Buns	___	___	___
	___	___	___
	___	___	___

	Qty	Cost	Cp
PAPER GOODS			
Paper Towels	___	___	___
Facial Tissue	___	___	___
Toilet Paper	___	___	___
Napkins	___	___	___
Plastic Wrap	___	___	___
Waxed Paper	___	___	___
Foil	___	___	___
Trash Bags	___	___	___
Zip Bags			
Small	___	___	___
Large	___	___	___
	___	___	___
	___	___	___
	___	___	___
HOUSEHOLD			
Dishwasher			
Soap	___	___	___
Dish Soap	___	___	___
Clothes Soap	___	___	___
Bleach			
White	___	___	___
Colors	___	___	___
Fabric			
Softener	___	___	___
Furniture			
Polish	___	___	___
Light Bulbs	___	___	___
Vacuum Bags	___	___	___
Pet Food	___	___	___
	___	___	___
	___	___	___
	___	___	___
	___	___	___
	___	___	___
	___	___	___
	___	___	___
	___	___	___
MEAT			
Beef	___	___	___
Chicken	___	___	___
	___	___	___
	___	___	___
	___	___	___
Fish	___	___	___
	___	___	___
	___	___	___

*cp = coupon

	Qty	Cost	Cp
DAIRY			
Milk	___	___	___
Butter	___	___	
Cheese	___	___	___
___	___	___	___
Eggs	___	___	___
Cottage Cheese	___	___	___
Sour Cream	___	___	___
Yogurt	___	___	___
___	___	___	___
___	___	___	___
___	___	___	___
FRESH PRODUCE			
Vegetables	___	___	___
___	___	___	___
Fruit	___	___	___
___	___	___	___
___	___	___	___
___	___	___	___
___	___	___	___
___	___	___	___
___	___	___	___
___	___	___	___
INTERNATIONAL FOODS			
Chinese	___	___	___
___	___	___	___
___	___	___	___
Mexican	___	___	___
___	___	___	___
___	___	___	___
Italian	___	___	___
___	___	___	___
___	___	___	___
___	___	___	___
___	___	___	___
DELI			
Sliced Meats	___	___	___
___	___	___	___
___	___	___	___
___	___	___	___
___	___	___	___
___	___	___	___

	Qty	Cost	Cp
Cheese			
Yellow	___	___	___
___	___	___	___
White	___	___	___
___	___	___	___
___	___	___	___
Prepared Salads	___	___	___
___	___	___	___
___	___	___	___
___	___	___	___
___	___	___	___
___	___	___	___
___	___	___	___
BAKERY			
Sweet Rolls	___	___	___
Cake	___	___	___
Doughnuts	___	___	___
Pies	___	___	___
Cookies	___	___	___
___	___	___	___
___	___	___	___
___	___	___	___
___	___	___	___
___	___	___	___
SCHOOL & OFFICE			
Pens	___	___	___
Pencils	___	___	___
Paper	___	___	___
Notebooks	___	___	
3 x 5 Cards	___	___	___
___	___	___	___
___	___	___	___
___	___	___	___
___	___	___	___
___	___	___	___
___	___	___	___
PERSONAL ITEMS			
Makeup	___	___	___
___	___	___	___
___	___	___	___
___	___	___	___
___	___	___	___
___	___	___	___

	Qty	Cost	Cp
PERSONAL ITEMS (cont.)			
___	___	___	___
___	___	___	___
Toothpaste	___	___	___
Deodorant	___	___	___
Hair Care	___	___	___
Hand Soap	___	___	___
Facial Cleaner	___	___	___
Feminine Protection	___	___	___
Razors	___	___	___
Shaving Cream	___	___	___
___	___	___	___
___	___	___	___
___	___	___	___
___	___	___	___
___	___	___	___
___	___	___	___
___	___	___	___
___	___	___	___
___	___	___	___
___	___	___	___
___	___	___	___
___	___	___	___
___	___	___	___
___	___	___	___
___	___	___	___
___	___	___	___
___	___	___	___
___	___	___	___
___	___	___	___
___	___	___	___
___	___	___	___
___	___	___	___
___	___	___	___
___	___	___	___
___	___	___	___
___	___	___	___

Let's Talk About Finances and Budgets

Getting Ready

Plan

Make certain that your young friend has indeed planned to meet with you and knows the time and place.

Prepare

Read Philippians 4:11,12; Matthew 5:14; 1 Timothy 6:18; Matthew 25:24-30

Read and meditate on the Scriptures listed above. Any material you have in your resources by Larry Burkett (*What Husbands Wish Their Wives Knew About Money* [Victor]) or Ron Blue (*Master Your Money* [Nelson]), both excellent money managers who write on the topic from a Christian perspective, will be helpful. If you do not manage the household budget in your family, talk to a few people who do handle the budgeting, purchasing, and bill-paying in their homes. Reflect on your own spending and saving practices.

Pray

Lord, help me to see and understand the different sides of this issue. Is money for spending or saving? Is there a balance presented in Your Word that will provide an answer? Am I a good steward, as described in Matthew?

Be Practical

If you use a budgeting system, be prepared to share it during your time together. If not, you will be able to find a sample budget worksheet in any of Larry Burkett's or Ron Blue's books.

Our Time Together

Warm Up

Review last session's topic, then get a feel for the way your young friend handles her finances. Remember that money is a very personal topic to discuss with anyone, so be sensitive.

Sharing Your Thoughts

This is a truly perfect time to talk priorities. It is important to establish how we consume our two great tangible resources: time and money. The heart of the issue regarding money is stewardship. We all need to understand that we own nothing. All we have is a gift from God, and He can do whatever He desires with His possessions. Our responsibility as stewards is to use all He has entrusted to us to bring glory to Him. This concept seems simple, but it is difficult, at best, to accomplish.

As stewards we are tasked with saving, investing, giving, and spending. Try to help your young friend discover for herself if she handles each of these areas equally well. If not, with which area does she have the most difficulty? Suggest how her training and experience may have contributed to her attitude toward finances. Also, present the format for establishing a budget if her family does not already use one.

Questions to Ponder

1. How did your parents handle money? Were they in agreement?

2. At what age were you given a degree of responsibility to handle money?

3. In terms of finances, do you think God is disappointed with you in any one area? If so, which area?

4. Do you and your husband agree on money matters? If not, what stands in the way of your agreement? Can you effect change?

5. Is there a maximum amount of money you can spend without consulting your husband? If finances are tight, you may find it helpful to establish a specific dollar amount as a ceiling of spending in your household.

Praying for Each Other

This topic may open the floodgates. Ask the Lord for honesty as you consider whether you tend to buy things in an attempt to satisfy another needy area in your life. Ask Jesus to replace any faulty financial philosophy with biblical thinking.

Growing Together

1. Chose your next topic, time, and location.

2. Decide if you want to commit to any specific change in the area of finances. For example, before making a purchase you could ask yourself, "Do I really need this, or do I just want it?"

3. Pray together. The needs we try to meet with money are enormous. Take time to ask God to help you be wise and careful with the resources He has given you permission to use.

❧ Mentoring Moment ❧

MR. & MRS. AVERAGE COUPLE

"Imagine a couple that doesn't operate on a margin. As so many couples do today, they follow the great American way, which is to buy things you don't need, with money you don't have, from the people you don't even like. They get themselves in a situation where they are overextended, and they have more obligations than they do income. Along the way, they've taken under their wing the support of their local church and some friends who have gone to the mission field. What happens? Well, pretty soon they find that they can't meet those missionaries' needs, and they can't give to their local ministry. Then maybe they get to the place where they face bankruptcy, the loss of the car, the loss of the house, the loss of the job, and the loss of their testimony. Now they are limited as to what they can do for God because they have to pay for their foolishness with every dime they get. If God ever came to them and called them away to some mission field, they could not go."

— JOHN MACARTHUR

Let's Talk About Feathering Your Nest

Getting Ready

Refer to sessions in this book on finances and organization.

Plan

Make certain that your young friend remembers the arrangements and assignments for the coming session.

Prepare

Read Proverbs 31

Read and meditate on the Scripture above. This session will present an opportunity for the two of you to have fun "talking house." Share about the time you painted your bedroom a lovely shade of soft pink that dried "hot pink"! Commiserate about putting up with the wrong color of carpet until it wears out. Remember a time when God asked you to wait for what you wanted and another time when God let you go first class.

Pray

Lord, help me to effectively communicate Your perspective on our earthly dwellings. May we learn to "feather our nests" without overdoing it.

Be Practical

Head for the library or magazine stand to find home decorating publications with inspiring pictures and tips for decorating on a budget. Find practical articles on such subjects as how to cover ceramic tile without buying new tile. If you have a friend in the interior design business, borrow some fabric books or consult her expertise for ideas to share with your young friend ... even if the only result is that one of you moves a picture to achieve a more pleasing visual effect. Keep in mind that your daughter-in-the-Lord may know more than you do about design. Give her the chance to shine!

Our Time Together

Warm Up

After reviewing your topic from last meeting, ask your young friend to recall the houses or apartments she grew up in. Find out if they were city or country dwellings, and get a feel for the style she prefers.

Sharing Your Thoughts

Rely on your resources to give you design ideas for discussion, and then draw on your relationship as you talk about what makes a house a home. Building a warm, welcoming nest takes heart and love and a hand of grace, not necessarily a generous budget. Paint covers anything as easily (and more cheaply) as fabulous wallpapers can. Invite your young friend to ask herself if she has done all she can with her resources to feather her nest. Does it creatively express who she is and what she wants her family and friends to feel?

Questions to Ponder

1. How do you feel you could better manage your home? This is an excellent time to refer to related sessions that address organization, budgeting, and financial management.

2. Do you like having guests in your home? Are you comfortable feeding them whatever you can rustle up?

3. Do people often tell you how welcome they feel in your home? If not, can you explain why not?

4. Have you ever transformed a room from ugly to beautiful? If so, take time to share the experience.

5. Are there little things you know that could be done right now to "feather up" your nest? Each of you make a list and share it.

Praying for Each Other

Share with the Lord your desires and frustrations about creating a pleasant home environment. Ask the Creator of all things to bring ideas and resources into your mind that will fit into your budget of time and money.

Growing Together

1. Choose your next meeting place, time, and topic, and look for any advance assignments.

2. The two of you might like to tackle a project together. Perhaps you both have silk flower arrangements that need to be refreshed or furniture that could be arranged to better advantage. Set a time when you can help each other accomplish the task you select.

3. Pray together. Rejoice in the common womanly challenge of trying to make a house a home. If money is no object, it is possible to buy lots of stuff and still fail to make people comfortable in your environment. If there is little money to spare, it is easy to forget that no more than a small piece of bright fabric will dress a table and set a cheerful mood for your next family meal.

❧ Mentoring Moment ☙

"Take comfort from what the famous designer Mary Gilliatt said, 'Too perfect rooms are as boring as too perfect people.' Try your wings."

— KAY EMERY, DESIGNER

Let's Talk About Creating Family Memories

Getting Ready

Plan
Confirm the time and place of your next meeting and ask your younger partner to come prepared to talk about meaningful traditions in her family.

Prepare
Read Psalm 22:2; 112:6; Isaiah 49:15; Luke 12:11,12; Hebrews 2:1;
Let's Make Memories *by Gloria Gaither and Shirley Dobson;* 15-Minute Family Traditions and Memories, *by Emilie Barnes; and my book,* Get More Done in Less Time.

Read and meditate on the Scriptures listed above. Tie these references to others you know in God's Word that encourage creating memories for the purpose of recording and recalling special events. Think about some memories you have created for others and those you treasure for yourself.

Pray
Lord, I want to remember You first and foremost. Whenever I partake of the communion table, let me be truly commemorating You and Your great gift to me. From this example help me to create memories in the lives of my loved ones.

Be Practical
You need time and perseverance in the face of obstacles when you attempt to create memories. Consider the time and effort it takes to prepare for a surprise party, wedding, or other major

event that is designed to create memories. At the same time, remember that the small traditions of the home are equally important.

Our Time Together
Warm Up
After reviewing last session's topic, ask your dear daughter-of-the-heart about her memories of childhood, school days, and courtship. Point out that there is usually a key person responsible for planning a memory we cherish.

Sharing Your Thoughts
Your discussion of the special memories created by others will hopefully inspire this young woman to want to do the same for the people God has placed in her world. Each of us can give the gift of creating a memory. It can be as simple as piling sugar and cinnamon on toast every Saturday or as complicated as a surprise party with 400 guests. Holidays are great times to establish traditions: a favorite vegetable dish that you only make at Thanksgiving, the huge candle that shows up on everyone's birthday cake, or the Easter basket that reappears every year with the family's favorite treats. *Love is what makes the event.*

Perseverance may be required to push past the reserve of your husband or the embarrassment of your teenager. Be willing to run the risk of rejection—it's worth it!

Questions to Ponder
1. Have you been hesitant to try to create a memory for someone who has rejected your attempts in the past?

2. Are you willing to risk rejection to create a memory that might bring a smile to someone's heart?

3. What would keep you from exerting the energy necessary to create a memory?

4. Discuss the Scripture passages that talk about remembering.

5. Have you ever wished that the family you grew up in had more traditions? Explain. Does this make you want to create memories for your loved ones, or does it make you afraid to try?

Praying for Each Other

During this session, you can talk about communion and how it helps us remember Jesus' death for our sins. If your church provides for its members to take communion together away from the church, that would be a memorable way to end this session.

Growing Together

1. Select your location, time, topic, and assignments for the coming session.

2. The two of you might enjoy planning a memory-making event together. Consult your calendars. Is there a holiday coming soon that would be useful as a starting point to plan a new tradition in your families? If not, make up a reason and plan away!

3. Pray together before you part.

❧ Mentoring Moment ❧

"Every meeting of persons is a unique exchange of gifts."
— RUEL HOWELL

Praying for Your Children

1. Pray that your children will fear the Lord and serve Him: "You shall fear only the Lord your God; and you shall worship Him, and swear by His name" (Deuteronomy 6:13 NASB).

2. Pray that your children will know Christ as Savior early in life: "O God, Thou art My God; I shall seek Thee earnestly; My soul thirsts for Thee, my flesh yearns for Thee, in a dry and weary land where there is no water" (Psalm 63:1NASB).

3. Pray that your children will hate sin: "Hate evil, you who love the Lord, who preserves the souls of His godly ones; He delivers them from the hand of the wicked" (Psalm 97:10 NASB).

4. Pray that your children will be caught when they're guilty: "It is good for me that I was afflicted, that I may learn Thy statutes" (Psalm 119:71 NASB).

5. Pray that your children will have a responsible attitude in all their interpersonal relationships: "Then this Daniel began distinguishing himself among the commissioners and satraps because he possessed an extraordinary spirit, and the king planned to appoint him over the entire kingdom" (Daniel 6:3 NASB).

6. Pray that your children will respect those in authority over them: "Let every person be in subjection to the governing authorities. For there is no authority except from God, and those which exist are established by God" (Romans 13:1 NASB).

7. Pray that your children will desire the right kind of friends and be protected from the wrong kind: "My son, if sinners entice you, do not consent. . . . Do not walk in the way with them. Keep your feet from their path" (Proverbs 1:10,15 NASB).

8. Pray that your children will be kept from the wrong mate and saved for the right one: "Do not be bound together with unbelievers; for what partnership have righteousness and lawlessness, or what fellowship has light with darkness" (2 Corinthians 6:14 NASB).

9. Pray that your children and their prospective mates will be kept pure until marriage: "Flee immorality. . . . Do you not know that your body is a temple of the Holy Spirit who is in you, whom you have from God, and that you are not your own? For you have been bought with a price: therefore glorify God in your body" (1 Corinthians 6:18-20 NASB).

10. Pray that your children will learn to submit totally to God and actively resist Satan in all circumstances: "Submit therefore to God. Resist the devil and he will flee from you" (James 4:7 NASB).

11. Pray that your children will be single-hearted, willing to be sold out to Jesus: "I urge you therefore, brethren, by the mercies of God, to present your bodies a living and holy sacrifice, acceptable to God, which is your spiritual service of worship. And do not be conformed to this world, but be transformed by the renewing of your mind, that you may prove what the will of God is, that which is good and acceptable and perfect" (Romans 12:1,2 NASB).

12. Pray that your children will be hedged in so they cannot find their way to wrong people or wrong places, and that wrong people cannot find their way to your children: "Therefore, behold, I will hedge up her way with thorns, and I will build a wall against her so that she cannot find her paths. And she will pursue her lovers, but she will not overtake them; and she will seek them, but will not find them" (Hosea 2:6,7 NASB).

13. Pray that your children will have quick, repentant hearts: "Be gracious to me, O God, according to Thy lovingkindness; according to the greatness of Thy compassion blot out my transgressions. Wash me thoroughly from my iniquity, and cleanse me from my sin. For I know my transgressions, and my sin is ever before me" (Psalm 51:1-3 NASB).

14. Pray that your children will honor their parents so all will go well with them: "Children, obey your parents in the Lord, for this is right. Honor your father and mother (which is the first commandment with a promise), that it may be well with you, and that you may live long on the earth" (Ephesians 6:1-3 NASB).

15. Pray that your children will be teachable and able to take correction: "And all your sons will be taught of the Lord; and the well-being of your sons will be great" (Isaiah 54:13 NASB); "A wise son accepts his father's discipline, but a scoffer does not listen to rebuke" (Proverbs 13:1 NASB).

16. Pray that your children's lives will bear the fruit of the Spirit: "The fruit of the Spirit is love, joy, peace, patience, kindness, goodness, faithfulness, gentleness, self-control; against such things there is no law" (Galatians 5:22,23 NASB).

17. Pray that your children will live by the Spirit and not gratify their flesh: "Walk by the Spirit, and you will not carry out the desire of the flesh" (Galatians 5:16 NASB).

18. Pray that your children will trust in the Lord for direction in their lives, including their occupation: "Trust in the Lord with all your heart, and do not lean on your own understanding. In all your ways acknowledge Him, and He will make your paths straight" (Proverbs 3:5,6 NASB).

Supplemental Reading List

15-Minute Family Traditions and Memories, Emilie Barnes, published by Harvest House.

Discover Your Children's Gifts, Doug and Katie Fortune, published by Chosen Books.

Fit to Be Tied, Bill Hybels, an audiotape distributed by Willow Creek Community Church, Barrington, Illinois.

Get More Done in Less Time, Donna Otto, published by Harvest House.

His Needs, Her Needs, Neil Harley, published by Revell.

The Language of Love, Gary Smalley and John Trent, published by Focus on the Family.

Let's Make Memories, Gloria Gaither and Shirley Dobson, published by Word.

The Marriage Builder, Larry Crabb, published by Zondervan.

Master Your Money, Ron Blue, published by Thomas Nelson.

Open Heart, Open Home, Karen Mains, published by Zondervan.

Please Understand Me, Kiersey Bates, published by Prometheus Nemesis Book Company.

The Power of a Praying Parent, Stormie Omartian, published by Harvest House.

The Stay-At-Home Mom, Donna Otto, published by Harvest House.

Two Sides of Love, John Trent, published by Focus on the Family.

They Didn't Know They Were Angels, Doris Greig, published by Regal Books.

The Treasure Tree, John Trent, published by Word.

What Husbands Wish Their Wives Knew About Money, Larry Burkett, published by Victor.

What Is a Family? Edith Schaeffer, published by Revell.

Additional Recommendations

1. *Discipline: The Great Surrender,* Elisabeth Elliot, published by Revell.

2. *Hints on Child Training,* H. Clay Trumbull, published by Wolgemuth & Hyatt.

3. *Me Obey Him?* Elizabeth Rice Handford, published by Sword of the Lord.

4. *The Shaping of a Christian Family,* Elisabeth Elliot, published by Thomas Nelson.

Resources for Women

BY DONNA OTTO

Mentors for Mothers is a one-of-a-kind program designed to establish vital relationships between older women who desire a significant ministry and younger women who need the encouragement and a role model that only an older woman can provide.

Program Manual

Entire package of material designed for the implementation of the program into the church curriculum. Materials for the 24-week program (and instructions on streamlining to a condensed 14-week plan) with job descriptions and instructions for the Director, Lead Teacher, Administrator, and Student are presented in a three-ring binder. An added extra is a helpful and concise taped message from the author. Only one program manual is needed to begin this timely, effective, and strengthening program in your church.
Available July 1998...$49.95

Participant Workbook

Designed specifically with the student in mind, this useful material contains outlines of the 24 weeks' study materials with titles, Scripture references, and life application directives. Includes necessary forms, a section of insights on getting to know your mentor, and adequate space for notes for each lesson.

Participant Workbook................ $5.50
Package of ten...........................$53.50

Between Women of God

In today's fast-paced, challenging world we still need times of refreshment and spiritual encouragement. Donna's book provides a perspective on the biblical mandate for women to care for the needs of other women. Inspirational and helpful to those who feel called to this important iministry or to younger women who desire mature discipleship. $8.99

The Stay-At-Home Mom, Revixed and Expanded

A wonderful presentation of the challenges and rewards facing today's mother who chooses to work inside the home rather than to work out in the world. Helpful ideas on managing the household, coping with the isolation that sometimes accompanies staying at home, and thoughts on some of the social/ financial pressures of staying at home. $8.99

Get More Done in Less Time

Break free from the all-work-and-no-play lifestyle with this practical, creative timesaving system to help you deal with clutter, deadlines, interruptions, budgets, and more. A passport to happier, healthier, and more relaxed living. $8.99

Dramatization

A 15-minute, 2-character sketch that portrays the work and rewards of mentoring. Great tool for motivating your women to get involved $5.00

Other Books, Tapes, and Supplies
BY DONNA OTTO

Time Maker Organizer & Refills
Vinyl Binder $52.95
Leather Binder $62.95

Mentors for Mothers
Notes, 50 per package $3.00
Prayer Page, 50 per package $3.00
Binder for Participant Workbook $3.50

PRICES SUBJECT TO CHANGE

	OFFICE USE ONLY	❑ Yes
	Ship Date _____	❑ No

✀ Order Form

	PRICE	QTY	TOTAL
MENTORS FOR MOTHERS			
Program Manual	$49.95	_____	_____
Participant Workbook	$5.50	_____	_____
Package of Ten	$53.50	_____	_____
Between Women of God	$8.99	_____	_____
The Stay-At-Home Mom	$8.99	_____	_____
The Gentle Art of Mentoring	$6.99	_____	_____
Dramatization	$5.00	_____	_____

Other Books and Tapes by Donna Otto

	PRICE	QTY	TOTAL
Get More Done in Less Time	$8.99	_____	_____
TIME MAKER ORGANIZER & REFILL			
Vinyl Binder	$52.95	_____	_____
Leather Binder	$62.95	_____	_____
MENTORS FOR MOTHERS			
Notes, 50 per package	$3.00	_____	_____
Prayer Page, 50 per package	$3.00	_____	_____
Binder for Student Manual	$3.50	_____	_____

MAKE CHECK PAYABLE TO: **Donna Otto**
11453 North 53rd Place
Scottsdale, AZ 85254
(602) 991-7464

Subtotal	_____
Sales Tax	_____
15% S/H ($2.25 min.)	_____
TOTAL	_____

Name_____ Phone (____) _____

Address_____ City_____ State____ Zip_____

Name of Organization, if applicable_____

Thank you for your order. If you have any questions, please feel free to call. We welcome your suggestions and recommendations.

Other Good Harvest House Reading

BETWEEN WOMEN OF GOD
by *Donna Otto*

With the hope of seeing the rich rewards and genuine fruit of godly wisdom blossom in women, Otto describes the Titus 2 relationship she has shared with Elisabeth Elliot. This book outlines ways to get involved in a special, encouraging mentor relationship.

GET MORE DONE IN LESS TIME
by *Donna Otto*

Break free from the all-work-and-no-play lifestyle with this practical, creative timesaving system to help you deal with clutter, deadlines, interruptions, budgets, and more. A passport to happier, healthier, and more relaxed living.

THE STAY-AT-HOME MOM
by *Donna Otto*

The stay-at-home mom deserves a book that applauds her choice. Donna's contagious warmth and boundless enthusiasm for home and personal organization overflow in this practical guide to living out the magic moments of motherhood.

FILL MY CUP, LORD
by *Emilie Barnes*

Bestselling author Emilie Barnes offers heartwarming meditations to help women find quietness and peace in today's world. From trials to triumph, she shares the comfort, peace, and thanksgiving found in our gracious Savior.

A WOMAN AFTER GOD'S OWN HEART
by *Elizabeth George*

Elizabeth George offers Scripture-based principles to every reader who wants to become God's woman of excellence. This is the book for any woman who wants to achieve a growing relationship with God, develop an active partnership with her husband, and make her home a spiritual oasis. Includes a study guide perfect for individual or group use.

Dear Reader,

We would appreciate hearing from you regarding this Harvest House nonfiction book. It will enable us to continue to give you the best in Christian publishing.

1. What most influenced you to purchase *The Gentle Art of Mentoring*?
   - ❑ Author
   - ❑ Subject matter
   - ❑ Backcover copy
   - ❑ Recommendations
   - ❑ Cover/Title
   - ❑ Other_____

2. Where did you purchase this book?
   - ❑ Christian bookstore
   - ❑ General bookstore
   - ❑ Department store
   - ❑ Grocery store
   - ❑ Other_____

3. Your overall rating of this book?
   ❑ Excellent   ❑ Very good   ❑ Good   ❑ Fair   ❑ Poor

4. How likely would you be to purchase other books by this author?
   ❑ Very likely   ❑ Not very likely   ❑ Somewhat likely   ❑ Not at all

5. What types of books most interest you? (Check all that apply.)
   - ❑ Women's Books
   - ❑ Marriage Books
   - ❑ Current Issues
   - ❑ Christian Living
   - ❑ Bible Studies
   - ❑ Fiction
   - ❑ Biographies
   - ❑ Children's Books
   - ❑ Youth Books
   - ❑ Other_____

6. Please check the box next to your age group.
   ❑ Under 18 ❑ 18-24 ❑ 25-34 ❑ 35-44 ❑ 45-54 ❑ 55 and over

Mail to: Editorial Director
Harvest House Publishers
1075 Arrowsmith
Eugene, OR 97402

Name_____

Address _____

State _____ Zip _____

Thank you for helping us to help you in future publications!